LIMITLESS LEADERSHIP

Limitless Leadership

Empowering Women to Unleash Their Potential & Rewrite the Rules for Success

©2025 All Rights Reserved. No portion of this book may be reproduced, stored in a retrieval system, or transmitted in any form or by any means—electronic, mechanical, photocopy, recording, scanning, or other—except for brief quotations in critical reviews or articles without the prior permission of the author.

Published by Game Changer Publishing

Paperback ISBN: 978-1-967424-22-1

Hardcover ISBN: 978-1-967424-23-8

Digital ISBN: 978-1-967424-24-5

www.GameChangerPublishing.com

LIMITLESS LEADERSHIP

Empowering Women to Unleash Their Potential &
Rewrite the Rules for Success

Foreword

BY CRIS CAWLEY

Leadership is not about titles, power, or authority—it is about impact, influence, and the ability to inspire others to rise. And yet, for too long, women in leadership have faced challenges that limit their full potential. *Limitless Leadership* is a testament to the truth that leadership has no ceiling when women step fully into their power.

In a world that is rapidly evolving, the need for strong, visionary female leaders has never been greater. This book is not just about breaking glass ceilings; it is about redefining leadership itself. It provides the strategies, insights, and mindset shifts necessary for women to lead with confidence, authenticity, and boldness—no matter the industry or stage of their journey.

As you turn the pages, you will discover the principles that set exceptional leaders apart. You will gain the tools to navigate challenges, own your voice, and build a leadership legacy that extends beyond professional success. Most importantly, you will be reminded that leadership is not a destination but a continuous journey of growth and impact.

The world needs more women who lead without limits. *Limitless Leadership* is your guide to becoming one of them.

Contents

Shattering Limits and Rising from the Ashes *By Danielle Maur*	1
No: Your Greatest Navigator *By Earlene Camielle*	15
D.R.E.A.M. in Motion *By Dr. Gina Kuhn-Robatin*	29
Lead Within to Lead Beyond *By Heidi Meckley*	41
Branding With Soul, Leading With Impact *By Katie Smetherman Holmes*	59
Unapologetically Thriving *By Kristin Kee*	71
The Chakra Codes: Unlock Your Rich Girl Energy *By Marissa Auloure*	85
Leading From Within *By Marissa Yubas*	117
Beyond the Racquet *By Tasha Doucas*	133
The Balance Behind the Breakthrough *By Tia Smith*	159

Shattering Limits and Rising from the Ashes

BY DANIELLE MAUR

I never imagined my life could change in the space of a single heartbeat. One moment, I am a corporate high-flyer, traveling the world and leading high-stakes projects with ease and confidence. The next, I am lying in a hospital bed, struggling to see the room that surrounded me through my distorted vision; my words were mumbled and slurred, like the slow stumbling speech of someone who had five too many. A devastating stroke had nearly claimed my life, and in one swift blow, all the authority and productivity that had once defined me seemed to vanish. I felt exiled to a foreign land—unable to speak the language or navigate the terrain.

You may not have faced something as traumatic as a stroke, but what happens when life forces you to confront your limits in ways you never expected? Hidden within my story is a powerful lesson about rising above life's greatest challenges to unlock the secrets of limitless leadership—and I promise, it's something that will help you, too.

In those early days, my mind could not compute how drastically my world had changed. I was used to measuring my worth by measurable achievements: closed deals, successful presentations, team morale, and bottom-line growth. Now my biggest accomplishment on any given day might be pronouncing a single syllable correctly or maintaining my balance long enough to walk a few steps down the hospital corridor without falling or crashing into anything. Where I once breezed through airports and conference rooms, I now dragged through my home feeling unsafe and unrecognizable; it became a tug-of-war between my body and my will.

I would be lying if I said I faced this new reality with immediate courage and grace. My first reaction was denial. *This cannot be me. This cannot be my life.* I kept thinking that at any moment, I would snap out of this nightmare, jump out of bed (like it was a cold), and return to business as usual. But the days rolled on, and that "business as usual" never arrived. Instead, there were doctors telling me that I wouldn't get better, telling me that this was only the beginning because most stroke victims have another stroke and die. And there I was; I now had a fearsome sense of guilt gnawing at my insides.

Why guilt? At first, this felt like a personal failure—I was an executive in the fitness industry, and now I was hearing statements like "You are what you eat," like I caused this through self-negligence. Did I really "eat" a stroke? I scolded myself: *How could I have let this happen?* But over time, another realization dawned on me, something that would eventually become the cornerstone of my new philosophy: *It's not about what you eat; it's about what you think.* In other words, the beliefs we choose to dwell on, the mindset we adopt, and the stories we tell ourselves each day are far more critical to our holistic well-being than any single aspect of nutrition or exercise. I came to believe that *you are what you think* and to become truly limitless, you must believe—deep down—that you *are* limitless.

In the weeks and months that followed my stroke, I had a lot of time to reflect. My mind churned like a powerful engine, still searching for a destination. *Who was I now, if not the corporate success story? Who was I if I couldn't speak, present, or negotiate deals in the boardroom? It was like meeting myself for the first time. A new identity was being born.*

This identity crisis was profound. I had built my entire self-image around professional competence and career accolades. My posture, handshake, and tone of voice all carried the confidence of someone who excelled in business. Yet, now here I was, with shaky limbs, fuzzy memories, double vision, and slurred speech. I suddenly felt incompetent, useless, broken—and even ashamed. It was as though the foundation of my identity had been hit by an earthquake, leaving a jagged fault line right through the middle of my self-esteem.

Once I was comfortable enough to move around my house, the real work of recovery began. Every morning, I would wake up to a sense of dread mixed with stubborn determination. I refused to let the doctors define my recovery or my future, so I would shuffle around the house with my heart pounding because I never knew if this would be the day I'd make progress or fall flat on my face. I fell so many times that it became a game. I put together simple exercises like repeating the alphabet, playing memory games, doing visual exercises, or balancing on one foot, and it became a monumental achievement if I managed it. Each success was a cause for celebration, but each failure felt like a dagger in my already wounded pride, and there would be many.

And yet, through the haze of medication, fear, and uncertainty, I could sense something new emerging: a flicker of possibility. It started small—like a glimmer of light at the end of a very long, dark tunnel. Whenever I managed to pronounce a word more clearly than the day before, I realized *I can do this*. When I went from needing a walker to walking with no support, I recognized a pattern: With consistent effort and unwavering belief, my body responded. My brain, once compromised by the stroke, was still wired for adaptation. The ability of the brain to reroute signals and effectively rebuild itself after trauma is called neuroplasticity.

This sparked a revelation that would color every aspect of my life from that point on: If the brain can recover from a stroke through diligent practice and the power of belief, then what else could be possible if we apply the same principles to our personal and professional challenges? In other words, if I—and my battered central nervous system—could learn to speak, walk, and start to see again, might I also learn to transform other areas of my life through a similar combination of consistent action and unshakeable belief?

That question drove me. As my speech improved and my vision was shifting, I began to study—slowly at first—mindset, motivation, and resilience. I devoured stories of people who had overcome seemingly insurmountable obstacles, from life-threatening illnesses to catastrophic life events. A recognizable pattern emerged that echoed my own experience as I slowly started to recover: Every one of these survivors shared an internal dialogue that pushed them forward. They believed, often in defiance of all medical logic, that they *would* recover or succeed. The world could whisper doom, but they kept shouting possibility.

Suddenly, it made sense why my childhood catchphrase, "You are what you eat," was too narrow to define a life. Certainly, nutrition is vital, but so is the "food" we feed our minds—our thoughts, beliefs, and the stories we rehearse. It's the mindset, the lens through which we interpret events, that ultimately shapes our actions. If I had let fear and despair dominate my thoughts during my recovery, I might never have gotten out of that hospital bed. If I'd believed the stroke was a sentence to perpetual dependence, I would have surrendered to limitations rather than reach for new heights.

Embracing "You are what you think" was a game-changer. It wasn't an overnight realization. I still had days when my body trembled from the after-effects of the stroke, and my speech left me in tears. But deep inside, I clung to a belief that I was limitless and could push past my current boundaries with enough focus and faith. This notion that my thoughts could shape my reality acted like a guiding star through the darkness, leading me toward incremental victories and, eventually, a sense of wholeness I had feared I would never experience again.

Slowly, I went from feeling guilty and ashamed to seeing myself as a determined survivor. My self-talk evolved from *I hate myself* and *How could I be so weak—am I a burden to my family?* to *I will overcome this,* and *Each day, I'm getting stronger.* The shift may sound subtle, but it had monumental effects on my motivation, my emotional state, and even my physical healing. My family found hope in my optimism. As my own energy changed, my environment reflected that change back to me in the form of renewed support and belief from those around me.

My priorities began to shift. I was still the same person in many ways: driven, focused, and eager to achieve. But I had a different perspective. Where once I'd measured success by the size of my salary or the prestige of my projects, I now found meaning in simpler, more fundamental achievements—like having a coherent conversation, cooking a meal without losing my balance or cutting my fingers, and walking in the park without feeling drained. I reveled in small miracles, realizing that they were the pillars of a new, fulfilling life.

It was around this time that I discovered a deep, almost spiritual calling to help others navigate their own adversities. I started journaling about my experiences, capturing every moment of terror, triumph, frustration, and gratitude. The more I wrote, the more it became clear that my story was not just my story. It was a tapestry of lessons that could resonate with anyone struggling to overcome something daunting. Regardless of whatever a person's obstacle is, the core principle is the same: *We are often stronger than we think, and our mindset can be the key to unlocking that strength.*

One morning, while reading through my journal entries, I was struck by an idea that felt like lightning in my brain: *What if I could share these lessons through coaching?* I had years of leadership experience in the corporate world, and I understood how businesses—and the people who run them—thrive or fail based on the stories they tell themselves. I had many skill sets that I could share to lead fellow women entrepreneurs to success. I also knew that the dynamics of personal growth, resilience, and motivation are universal. A spark of excitement lit up my chest at the thought of guiding women to rewrite their own narratives—to show them that they could be limitless, too.

But it went deeper than just generic coaching. Throughout my career, I'd encountered countless women who struggled with self-doubt, systemic bias, work-life balance pressures, and a lingering feeling that they were not "enough"—not smart enough, not assertive enough, not worthy enough. Some were mothers trying to prove their competence in the corporate sphere. Others were professionals aiming to shatter glass ceilings but were sabotaged by their own beliefs. My own brush with mortality had illuminated something vital: If I, after a near-death experience, could rebuild my confidence and find a renewed sense of purpose, then anyone could. We just need the right tools, strategies, and support system.

Fueled by this clarity, I decided to become a business coach specifically for women, offering them the insights I had gleaned from both my corporate triumphs and my personal calamity. My mission is to help them discover the limitless power within, despite whatever setbacks or obstacles they might face. Perhaps it was a demanding job, a hidden health issue, or a fear of stepping into leadership positions. Whatever their limitations, I wanted to teach them that the only true limits are the ones we believe in and, therefore, impose on ourselves.

I poured myself into this new calling. I read voraciously about coaching methodologies, neuro-linguistic programming, positive psychology, and the science of resilience. The themes that resonated most strongly were those that emphasized the transformative power of mindset—reinforcing my belief that *you are what you think* is not just a platitude but a profound truth that can redefine one's life. I began crafting programs and strategies, blending corporate best practices with personal development techniques that centered on harnessing the power of one's own thoughts.

All the while, I drew on the raw, personal experiences of my stroke recovery to illustrate the deeper truths. When clients expressed fear about speaking up in meetings, I'd recall how I had struggled to speak at all—and how every syllable was a victory in the face of doubt. When someone felt guilty for needing help, I'd share how letting others assist me, from doctors to family members, had been my lifeline. And when people said they felt "too broken" to move forward, I would tell them about the nights I cried myself to sleep, feeling like a burden who would never return to "normal," only to awaken each morning with a renewed drive to keep going.

Throughout this journey, I refined and distilled the mindset strategies that had brought me from the brink of helplessness to a place of empowerment. These became the foundational blocks of my coaching approach and, ultimately, the basis for living a limitless life. I refer to them as the three core mindset strategies, and they are as follows:

1. Radical Acceptance

Radical acceptance is not about resignation or giving up; it's about recognizing reality as it is rather than as we wish it to be. When the stroke hit me, my initial response was denial: *This can't be happening to me.* That mental block slowed my early progress because I wasted precious emotional energy resisting the truth. Once I pivoted to acceptance—*yes, I've had a stroke; yes, I need support; yes, my brain is healing*—I was finally able to put all my energy into rehabilitation. Accepting the situation allowed me to focus on what I *could* do rather than lament what I couldn't.

I encourage anyone facing a challenge to pause and acknowledge the facts. It might feel uncomfortable and even painful, but acknowledging "what is" becomes the launch pad for moving toward "what can be." Whether it's a job loss, a health setback, a failed relationship, or the loss of a home, resisting the situation only prolongs the agony. Accept it, and then plan your way forward.

2. Reframe Every Setback as a Setup

Our instinct often is to view failure as a judgment on our worth, as though a setback says, *I am incapable, worthless, or doomed to repeat this.* But what if every misstep is, in fact, a setup—a lesson about what doesn't work, combined with a clue about how to course correct for next time? At the beginning of my recovery, I'd often slur my words or get frustrated when a sentence came out wrong.

Initially, this felt humiliating. But over time, I noticed patterns: I struggled most with certain consonants, or my speech improved when I slowed down. That wasn't failure; it was information guiding me to tweak my approach. It was a lesson. It was a setup.

When you adopt this mindset, every "defeat" becomes an experiment. Miss a deadline? The lesson tells you to adjust your time management. Had an unsuccessful job interview? The lesson suggests focusing on specific areas for improvement. This principle of reframing frees you from the emotional baggage of failure and transforms each challenge into a stepping stone.

3. Commit to a Higher Purpose

Healing and personal development are inherently meaningful, but they become even more powerful when tied to a larger goal. For me, the spark that propelled me through the darkest days of my stroke recovery was the idea that my journey could help others. I wanted to stand as a living testament that adversity, however overwhelming, doesn't define you. Whenever I felt like quitting, I'd remember the women I hoped to coach, the stories I aimed to tell, and the impact I wanted to make on a world that often underestimates female potential.

If you connect your progress to something bigger—whether that's inspiring your children, mentoring younger colleagues, contributing to your community, or addressing a social issue—your motivation gains an almost unbreakable quality. You're no longer fighting just for your own success or survival; you're striving for something that transcends your personal struggles.

Together, these three strategies form a powerful approach to cultivating what I now call the "limitless" mindset. It is a way of navigating the world with the conviction that you can rise above your current circumstances, no matter how dire they appear. Just as a seed, when planted in fertile soil, will push through layers of dirt toward the surface in search of sunlight, a limitless mindset insists on growth in the face of adversity.

This is not to say the journey is easy. There were times during my recovery when I felt I had taken three steps forward, only to tumble five steps back. I remember a particularly grueling week when, after making significant gains in my speech, I unexpectedly lost some progress. My words once again came out jumbled, and my fatigue was overwhelming. In moments like that, negative thoughts crept in: *Maybe I'll never fully recover. Maybe this is as far as I go.* But I had a choice to dwell on those thoughts or to push them aside and recall a better one—*I am what I think, and I think I can keep improving.* Over time, that unwavering belief proved more accurate than my passing fears.

It might sound simplistic, but maintaining that belief often required me to do battle with myself daily. I developed routines to reinforce positivity. I wrote affirmations every morning, practiced gratitude for every small victory, and limited my exposure to anything that fed my anxiety—be it news, social media, or even certain conversations. I was learning to guard my mind as carefully as one might guard a precious artifact. After all, if you are what you think, then what you allow into your mind—what you consume mentally—becomes critically important.

As I transformed my inner world, my outer world began to shift in remarkable ways. Friends and family who had initially been cautious about my fragility started to reflect my renewed sense of self back to me. They treated me less like a patient and more like a person on a mission. Opportunities to share my story began creeping up— an invitation to share my story on virtual platforms and in-person stages, podcasts, and with my first few clients. With each endeavor, my voice grew stronger and more deeply committed.

Through coaching these women, I realized that while everyone's story is unique, the underlying emotional currents are surprisingly similar. Many of my clients struggled with self-imposed limitations: "I'm too old to start a new career," or "I'm not smart enough to run my own business," or "I don't have the confidence to speak up in meetings." They were haunted by their own version of "You are what you eat"—some outdated rule or label they'd absorbed from childhood, telling them what they could or couldn't be. I found immense joy in guiding them to replace these limiting beliefs with empowering ones—teaching them, in essence, that *they are what they think*. And when they choose to think in terms of boundless possibility, incredible transformations can occur.

Over time, my work gained traction, and more women sought me out, often referred by friends who'd experienced their own breakthroughs. Some overcame their fear of public speaking and became advocates for causes dear to their hearts. Others left dead-end jobs to pursue entrepreneurial ventures they were passionate about. A few mended relationships by applying the same mindset strategies to emotional wounds that had lingered for years. In each case, the catalyst was a shift in thinking—from focusing on limitations to embracing infinite potential.

Looking back, I can see how my stroke, while nearly taking my life, also gave me life in an entirely new way. It forced me to confront my illusions of control and realize that physical health is just one layer of the equation. The deeper layer—the one that truly shapes our destinies—is our mindset. Without my stroke, I might never have understood the profound power of reframing challenges, nor would I have stepped onto the path of coaching and changing lives. The experience taught me empathy on a level I'd never known before, and it reminded me that adversity can be the gateway to a higher calling if we choose to see it that way.

When I reflect on my own evolution—from a corporate executive who secretly tied her self-worth to external achievements to someone who measures success by how much she can empower others—I realize that this transformation was possible only because I changed what I fed my mind. I stopped allowing fear, guilt, and shame to be the main ingredients in my mental diet. Instead, I nourished my thoughts with hope, purpose, and unwavering belief in limitless possibilities. That shift became the keystone that supported all other changes in my life.

And so, I invite you to examine the stories you tell yourself. Are they stories of scarcity and limitation or tales of abundance and potential? How do you see yourself when you strip away your titles, responsibilities, and external metrics of success? If you were lying in a hospital bed and forced to rebuild from scratch, what would you cling to as your source of strength? These are hard but essential questions because the answers will reveal the bedrock of your mindset—the place from which all your actions and reactions stem.

Know this: No matter your current challenges—be they financial, relational, physical, or emotional—you have within you the same capacity for resilience and rebirth. It may not be a stroke or a catastrophic event that jolts you into change; perhaps it's the quiet but persistent feeling that you're meant for something more. Either way, the principle remains: *What you think, you become.* If you believe you are limited, you'll live within the confines of those perceived limits. But if you dare to believe in your own limitlessness —even when the evidence around you is scarce—you open a door for transformation that might just lead you to your greatest fulfillment.

It's a lesson that stems all the way back to my childhood, where "You are what you eat" was drilled into me by well-meaning adults. I appreciate their intention; it taught me discipline and respect for my body. But over time, I recognized that the more profound truth lies in the realm of the mind. Yes, it matters what nourishment we give our physical selves, but it matters even more what beliefs we feed our consciousness, for it is within our own thoughts that the seeds of every possibility are planted.

I've often wondered how my younger self might have reacted had someone told me, "You are what you think. Feed your mind good stuff." I suspect I would have laughed, maybe found it too abstract. I was a practical, goal-oriented person; I liked tangible results and straightforward instructions, after all. Yet, here I am, living proof that the intangible realm of thought is where the most significant battles are fought and won. The stroke forced me to fight a battle I never expected, but it also led me to a discovery far more valuable than any corporate accolade: the knowledge that we are always in conversation with ourselves and that the nature of that conversation shapes everything else.

If, while reading this, you find yourself resonating with any part of my journey—maybe you've felt broken, maybe you've questioned your self-worth, or maybe you've been told you can't achieve something significant—I urge you to challenge those limiting beliefs. Think of them as old software in need of an update. You can install new programming anytime you choose, one that tells you, *I am capable, I am evolving, I am enough, and I am limitless.* The beauty of the human experience is that our minds are flexible, our beliefs moldable, and our stories are forever open to revision.

And this brings me full circle: In the days following my stroke, I felt like damaged goods. I thought I had let down everyone, including myself, by failing to maintain the robust health that had been my pride. But that self-blame, while perhaps a natural reaction, did not serve me. It did not propel me toward recovery or personal growth. Only when I embraced a new narrative—one that accepted my stroke as both a challenge and an invitation to transcend it—did I begin to heal in the deepest sense of the word. That healing went beyond my body. It mended my spirit, reoriented my life's purpose, and ignited a flame for guiding others toward their own limitless potential. The stroke was a gift.

Now, as I stand before you, offering my story and the mindset strategies that have reshaped my life, I do so with profound humility and unwavering conviction. Humility because I know how fragile life can be and how quickly it can change. Conviction because I have seen firsthand that a mindset anchored in limitless possibility can transform not just an individual but entire communities of people who become inspired to aim higher and do better.

My journey from fragile patient to resilient business coach was neither quick nor easy. However, it was rich with lessons that I believe can serve anyone willing to confront their fears, question their limitations, and open themselves to new dimensions of possibility.

If you take nothing else from this chapter, let it be this: **You are what you think.** Guard your thoughts as you would guard the most precious resource in your life because that's exactly what they are. Feed your mind with faith, with dreams, with knowledge that elevates your perspective, and with experiences that challenge you to grow. In doing so, you'll cultivate the fertile ground needed for your fullest potential to bloom.

It is my hope that by sharing my story, you will see reflections of your own strength—even if you haven't yet realized it. Because no matter what adversity you face, you hold within you an unbreakable and limitless spark. You can choose to fan that spark into a guiding flame, or you can let the winds of self-doubt extinguish it. I chose the flame, and it led me here—to a life of purpose, resilience, and the exhilarating pursuit of helping women entrepreneurs unlock and live in their own limitless power.

Danielle Maur is a trusted premier business coach specializing in proven, personalized business strategies that empower ambitious women entrepreneurs to unlock their full potential and master their mindset so they can build, launch, and scale their businesses with confidence.

With a results-driven approach, she transforms the way women think about success, helping them adopt high-performance habits that fuel limitless growth and long-term business success.

With over two decades of experience building 6-, 7-, and 8-figure businesses, Danielle understands that true success isn't just about strategy—it's also about mindset mastery.

She is devoted to crafting personalized, actionable game plans that align with each client's values, style, and goals, ensuring their business is as unique as they are.

Unlike cookie-cutter coaching programs, Danielle's no-fluff, no-BS approach helps entrepreneurs break through self-doubt, eliminate limiting beliefs, and build unshakable confidence. She believes that when you master your mindset, you unlock unlimited possibilities—in business, in leadership, and in life.

SHATTERING LIMITS AND RISING FROM THE ASHES

If you're an ambitious woman coach or entrepreneur ready to embrace your power, ditch the overwhelm, and achieve unstoppable momentum, Danielle is the game-changing coach you need.

Take the Next Step Toward Limitless Growth!

Visit: daniellemaur.com

Follow Danielle:

Facebook
@danielle.maur

Instagram
@daniellemaur

LinkedIn
@daniellemaur

No: Your Greatest Navigator

BY EARLENE CAMIELLE

I'm Earlene Camielle, a purpose and leadership coach, global speaker, and media and marketing strategist. In my career, I've had the privilege of helping individuals and leaders cultivate a mindset that empowers them to turn challenges into opportunities. Today, I want to focus on one of the most powerful and often misunderstood moments a leader can experience: encountering the word *no*.

This chapter is for you, the leaders who are making industry-shaping decisions, guiding teams through change, or pushing the boundaries of what's possible. If you've ever faced rejection, been told *no*, or felt that you or your vision was dismissed, this chapter will help you shift your mindset around those moments. My goal is to help you elevate how you approach the *no's* in your life and work and use them to propel you to greater success and clarity.

In the next few pages, I'll share insights and strategies that can transform how you view and react to a *no*. Let's dive into how to embrace *no* as a catalyst for growth, resilience, and leadership that breaks barriers. If you're ready to redefine your relationship with the word *no* and unlock your leadership potential, this chapter is for you.

No as Your Navigator: How to Use *No* to Find and Drive Solutions as a Leader

When we hear the word *no*, it sounds permanent, like a fixed answer to something that is no longer an option or possibility.

Oxford says that the word *no* as a noun is a negative answer or decision; as an adverb, it means not at all or to no extent.

This certainly sounds permanent, but I want to present the word *no* to you as an opportunity: In fact, it is one of life's rarest treasures that serves as a compass to point you in the right direction and keep you on your individual path as a leader in all areas of your life. Every *no* you've ever received or will receive can be used to elevate the skills you need to be a great leader.

Processing the *no's* you receive in a healthy way will build your decision-making and problem-solving skills, your adaptability and emotional intelligence, along with your resilience, confidence, and even negotiating and networking skills. Each *no* offers you the opportunity to grow and develop a stronger and more adaptable leadership style to get great results in your personal and professional life.

It has been proven[*] that the experiences we've encountered as children and young adults serve as the foundation for our value and belief systems, which inform how we receive and perceive things. That means that every time you received a *no* as a child, your experience and perception of this word tell you even today how to receive it. If most of your *no's* resulted in negative feelings and outcomes, subconsciously, you are still receiving and processing the *no's* you receive the same way you did back then when these *no's* are beautiful opportunities and great treasures for you to regroup, recalibrate, realign, build, and expand on who you are and what you want to achieve.

---

[*] Daines, C. L., Hansen, D., Novilla, M. L. B., & Crandall, A. (2021, April 5). Effects of positive and negative childhood experiences on adult family health - BMC public health. BioMed Central. https://bmcpublichealth.biomedcentral.com/articles/10.1186/s12889-021-10732-w

Using *no* as a navigational system looks similar to:

1. Missing Your Exit on a Roundabout: A delay that doesn't block progress but requires patience and focus.

There are moments when our journey doesn't go as planned. Similar to approaching a roundabout and missing your turn, these moments may initially feel frustrating, but they are not the end—they are opportunities for redirection. Missing a turn doesn't mean the journey is over. It's simply an invitation to loop around, take a moment to reassess, and then proceed with more insight and clarity.

Leaders face many *no's* and setbacks in their journey, just like a driver missing a turn in a roundabout. The key to leadership is in how we respond to these detours, choosing to navigate through them with resilience and flexibility, ultimately leading to even greater opportunities.

CEO of FarrBetter, Melanise Farrington, recently shared the power of redirection and detours and how a *no* can become an opportunity for growth. She shared:

> "In 2018, I pitched my services to a company to be their buyer. I knew they needed me, but when they said 'no,' I didn't give up—I saw it as just a missed turn. It felt like I had come to a roundabout and missed the exit I expected, but I wasn't ready to let it stop me. Instead of letting that 'no' block my progress, I looped around and took a different approach. I researched their needs and realized I had the products they were looking for. So, instead of trying to be hired as their buyer, I pitched to them the idea of purchasing those products from me directly."

> "If I hadn't received that 'no,' I might have ended up being an employee in their company. But instead, that setback became a pivot point that turned into an entrepreneurial opportunity. I went on to become one of Amazon's top sellers, introducing products like Oatly to the U.S. market. What I thought was a

setback was actually the detour I needed to find the path that truly aligned with my purpose."

Just like navigating a roundabout, leadership often requires us to loop back around after facing a *no* or a missed opportunity. It's not about being stuck or defeated—it's about re-evaluating, adjusting, and finding a new path forward. Melanise Farrington's story shows us that setbacks are often the beginning of something better. What may initially feel like a roadblock is simply an invitation to pause, reassess, and approach the journey with renewed focus.

In leadership, the ability to redirect, adapt, and embrace new opportunities is essential. Like a driver who misses their turn but takes the next loop to get it right, great leaders take each *no* and missed opportunity as a chance to realign their path and move forward with greater purpose and impact.

2. Hitting Rocky Terrain While Enjoying a Bike Ride

A sudden challenge that demands quick adjustments and persistence but doesn't stop you from moving forward.

Imagine taking a beautiful ride near the mountains. The path is clear, and you're able to enjoy the scenery and fresh mountain breeze. After about 15 minutes into your ride, you're faced with a change of scenery in the form of rocky terrain. At some point, you must have taken a wrong turn because this was not a part of your route. Your smooth ride all of a sudden becomes a ducking and dodging match between you and the bulldozer-sized rocks and medium-sized pebbles that your bike is continually jolted by. This was certainly unexpected and serves just a little too much uncertainty for you. The smooth, easy ride on good terrain represents the moments in life when things are going smoothly... Plans are progressing, goals are achievable, and everything feels aligned. But then, when rocky terrain with huge boulders suddenly appears, it mirrors the unexpected *no's* or setbacks that disrupt our course. Just like the rider would need to adjust quickly, maneuver, find a new path, or overcome physical obstacles, this analogy shows how we, too, must adapt quickly in response to challenges, reevaluating strategies and adjusting our mindset to keep moving forward.

Earla Bethel, a true trailblazer and franchise owner of a leading fast-food chain, exemplifies what it means to navigate challenges with unshakable resilience, grace, and determination. In late 2022, she faced a series of *no's* that threatened to derail the strategic plans and approvals she needed to propel her business forward. However, these setbacks didn't define her. Instead, Earla leaned into her faith, trusting that her path was guided by something greater.

Rather than letting the weight of rejection hold her back, Earla chose to rise above it. She confronted corporate and governmental barriers head-on, challenging those who stood in her way. Her courage and leadership transformed adversity into success, driving double-digit sales growth for twelve consecutive months. Earla reflects:

> *"By relying on my faith and trust in God, remaining resilient, and continually seeking solutions in the face of 'no's,' I achieved remarkable results. I surrendered my struggles to my Heavenly Father, knowing He fights for me, and it always turns out for my good and His Glory."*

As a leading lady in her industry, Earla embodies the power of resilience, faith, and leadership. She is a living example of what it means to face adversity head-on, turn setbacks into comebacks, and empower others to do the same. Her journey reminds us that no matter how many *no's* we face, we are capable of achieving great things with faith, determination, and the courage to keep moving forward.

3. Arriving at an Unexpected Fork in the Road

A decision that redirects your journey, reminding you that the right path might not always be the one you expected.

Just like a cyclist navigating smooth terrain suddenly faces an unexpected rocky path, sometimes life presents us with moments where our course is altered unexpectedly. But instead of seeing these shifts as roadblocks, we can view them as invitations to redirect our journey.

For many, receiving a *no* feels like reaching a fork in the road. Suddenly, the path we thought we were meant to take no longer seems possible or viable. The *no* acts as a prompt for us to choose a new direction. It's not an end but a pivotal moment of redirection, an opportunity to reassess, adjust, and take a path we may not have considered before.

Consider the moment when a driver reaches a fork in the road. The clear, straight path they were on is no longer an option. Left or right? The decision might seem very challenging, but it offers a chance to chart a new course. Just as the driver cannot predict every twist and turn ahead, we, too, must trust that, even with a new direction, we can still reach our desired destination.

Life often brings moments where a *no* isn't a rejection but rather a divine redirection, pushing us toward a path we may not have chosen but one that is ultimately meant for us. These pivotal moments, where we stand at a fork in the road, challenge us to trust in the greater purpose behind the obstacles we face.

I hold Councilman, Coach, and Pastor Ricardo Miller in the highest esteem. His journey is a profound example of how the *no's* we face in life are not always setbacks—they are often divine redirections that set us on a course toward unexpected blessings, growth, and purpose. His story beautifully illustrates the transformative power of embracing redirection. Ricardo shared with me:

"Years ago, I was told 'no' when I wanted to remain in the Bahamas to expand my national youth program, which at the time was flourishing. I had invested so much of myself into it and believed it was my path forward. But I was told 'no' and advised to move to the United States to launch the program there. At that moment, I resisted. The Bahamas was where my heart was, and it was difficult to understand why the path I envisioned for myself was being blocked. I couldn't see beyond the immediate disappointment.

Looking back, I now see how God used that 'no' to position me for something greater. It wasn't just about expanding my influence globally; it was about deepening my roots in the Bahamas in ways I never could have imagined. That 'no' wasn't a roadblock; it was the redirection I needed. It refined me and set me on a path that has shaped who I am today. What I initially thought was a setback was actually a setup for something much bigger."

Ricardo's decision to embrace the *no* and follow the redirection not only expanded his national platform but also opened doors to a global one, allowing him to positively impact people in over 15 countries. Today, he reflects with gratitude, saying, "I truly believe that some *'no's* are divine setups for our destiny, doors that God closes to guide us toward our true purpose."

Life's forks in the road are not signs of failure but invitations to redirect and grow in leadership. When we face a *no*, it's often a signal to pause, consider other paths, and trust that there are new routes to success that we might not have seen at first. Like the driver at the fork, we must trust that every direction holds lessons and possibilities, and it's our willingness to adjust that determines how far we can go and grow.

4. A Ship Caught in a Storm

A powerful disruption that forces you to navigate with resilience, knowing calmer waters are ahead.

Picture a ship sailing smoothly on calm seas. Let's say it's a cruise ship, and everyone on board has been enjoying the journey they've been on. There's been a planned itinerary, and each stop has been beautiful and rewarding. This cruise ship represents the times when our plans and efforts are progressing effortlessly, and everything feels like it's going as expected. On the third day of this trip, a dangerous, unpredictable storm presents itself and interrupts everything. This storm represents the unexpected *no's* that appear out of nowhere, threatening to derail our progress. Just like a captain has to adjust and navigate through rough waters to keep the ship steady during a storm, we must find the strength and strategies to stay on course when faced with rejection or setbacks, adjusting our approach and maintaining focus on the destination.

A dear friend and esteemed colleague, Anthia Butler, experienced an unexpected storm in the form of a *no* that she had to navigate with grace and resilience. Anthia, a seasoned leadership and operations expert, had dedicated seven years of her time and talent as the vice president of a company. She believed deeply in their vision and worked tirelessly to make a meaningful impact. Unexpectedly, she received an update that she was no longer needed in that role or at the company. This sudden *no* shook Anthia's world, as she had invested so much of herself in the company's growth and success.

Yet, in the face of this storm, Anthia didn't let the winds of disappointment blow her off course. Instead, she realized that this *no* wasn't an end but a redirection, a divine push toward a new and greater purpose. As she embraced the end of that season, she found herself free from a title and role that had begun to define and confine her. In her own words, she said:

"As that season came to an end, I embraced a path that was more purposeful and limitless. Now, I am being called to use that same time and talent I poured out in a way that aligns with God's greater plan for my life. Every closed door is His way of guiding me toward something greater for my good and His glory."

Anthia's story is a beautiful testament to the power of redirection. She says, "The best is yet to come," and urges us all to let the *"no"* prepare us for the *"new."*

Much like a ship sailing the vast ocean, life's journey is not always smooth sailing. When calm seas suddenly turn into stormy waters, and we face a *no* that seems to throw us off course, it's easy to feel disoriented. But just as a seasoned captain doesn't let the storm define the course of the ship, it's not the storm that defines us as leaders but how we navigate through it. By holding steady to the wheel with resilience, courage, and a clear sense of direction, we can weather any storm and continue forward, confident that each *no* is preparing us for something greater.

Anthia's testimony is a profound reminder that, as leaders, we have the ability to choose how we respond to the storms in our lives. We can either let them deter us or use them as opportunities to adjust our course and chart a new path. The storms of life will come, but with the right mindset, we can continue moving forward—stronger, wiser, and more aligned with our true purpose.

5. Waiting at a Delayed Stop Light

A pause that allows time for reflection, recalibration, and readiness for the next step in your journey.

In leadership, just as in life, *no's* can feel like roadblocks or delays. Imagine driving down the road and approaching a stoplight that turns red, forcing you to pause, and it takes forever to turn green. You're not stuck, but you must wait, sometimes longer than anticipated. This moment of delay can be frustrating, especially when we're eager to move forward. However, just as a red light gives us the chance to assess the situation, collect our thoughts, and prepare for the next phase of our journey, a *no* offers a similar opportunity.

A stoplight can be seen as a temporary pause, but in leadership, it can also represent a chance to regroup. It's in these moments of stillness that we can evaluate our options, adjust our strategy, and move forward with greater clarity and purpose. Rather than seeing delays as obstacles, leaders understand that they are moments for reflection, recalibration, and preparation for success ahead.

Someone that I admire greatly shared a pivotal *no* she received early in her life that helped to build her into the resilient and strong leader she is today. Senior Administrator Lorraine Elliot shared this testimony with me:

"Leading up to my high school graduation, everything seemed set for the next big step. I was ready to embark on my journey to college. I had been accepted to the University of Tennessee in Knoxville. I was filled with anticipation and excited to step into a new chapter of my life and pursue my studies. However, just one week before my departure, I was faced with devastating news from my father: There were no funds available to send me off to college. At that moment, I felt as though my dreams had come to a complete halt. Yet, despite the overwhelming disappointment, I refused to let this 'no' dictate my future.

Rather than allowing the setback to derail my aspirations, I took a deep breath and recalibrated. I chose to enroll at CR Walker Technical College, where I pursued a course in Secretarial Science. This decision, though initially a delay, became the catalyst for the career I would later build. It opened doors in the industries of tourism and banking, and eventually led me to the legal field, where I have spent much of my career. Looking back, I have no regrets. That 'no' was not the end of my journey; it was merely a pause, a redirection that set me on a path I might not have discovered otherwise. Today, I can look back and see how every step, every detour, and every lesson has been instrumental in my growth as both a professional and a leader."

Lorraine's testimony is a powerful example of resilience in the face of a *no*. When life handed her an unexpected setback, she adapted and chose to take a different route, allowing the experience to shape her into a well-rounded individual. This shift from disappointment to determination mirrors the journey of a leader, recognizing that setbacks are not permanent roadblocks but rather opportunities for redirection, growth, and unforeseen success. Just as Lorraine's experience opened doors she hadn't anticipated, leaders can find strength in recalibrating when faced with a *no*, trusting that the journey ahead will unfold in ways they may never have imagined.

In reflecting on my own journey as a leader, coach, strategist, mother, and child of God, I am grateful for every *no* or perceived *no* that I have encountered. Each one has set me up for a greater yes that I have been able to cultivate and maintain for a lifetime. Without those *no's*, I would not have gained the wisdom, understanding, strategies, endurance, and perseverance required to sustain and steward every yes that followed.

I have come to understand that the *no's* were not just external rejections; they were internal opportunities to process and heal from past experiences of rejection, neglect, and abandonment I faced in my childhood and young adulthood. These past traumas made me more sensitive to perceived rejections, often leading me to interpret even a delayed response as a *no*. However, in working to process my own reactions and understanding of how these past wounds showed up in different aspects of my life, incredible growth occurred that pushed me to my next level in leadership and yielded a healthier and more resilient woman.

This is why I've deemed *no's* as navigators rather than a source of defeat. I receive them as guideposts, pointing me toward the next opportunity and to the correct door that I'm supposed to walk through.

Each *no* is our chance to conquer limitations and rise above adversity. *No's* are not just obstacles; they are opportunities to regroup, rebuild, realign, re-establish, and recalibrate. They invite us to see what is needed to adjust our approach and work on exactly what is required to steward the yes ahead.

In this light, *no* becomes not an end but a pause, a moment to reflect and refine our vision, intentions, and strategy. It is an invitation to clarify our purpose and to reaffirm our commitment to the path ahead, even when the road feels uncertain. The *no's* help steer us in the right direction, allowing us to navigate more wisely toward the *yes* that is waiting for us.

If you're ready to dive deeper into developing your leadership mindset, I invite you to visit www.earlenecamielle.com for coaching services designed to help you elevate your purpose, confidence, and impact as a leader. You can also email me at ask@earlenecamielle.com. Let's work together to unlock the next level of success in your career and your life.

Thank you for investing your time in this chapter. I'm excited to guide you on this journey of transformation. Remember, every *no* is a stepping stone to your next breakthrough. I look forward to working with you to help you navigate the challenges ahead with confidence and clarity.

Earlene Camielle is an Award-Winning TV Show Host, Global Speaker, Coach, and Media and Marketing Strategist with a mission to inspire leaders to unlock their highest potential. Transitioning from a successful corporate career to embracing her purpose-driven path, Earlene now empowers professionals and entrepreneurs to pursue their vision with purpose, guiding them to lead with clarity and create great impact.

With expertise in project management, marketing, media, and entrepreneurship, Earlene's influence spans multiple industries, and her commitment to self-development fuels her drive to guide others. Through her coaching, she helps clients identify their unique strengths, build compelling personal brands, and craft strategic plans that propel their careers and businesses to new heights. Earlene is dedicated to helping leaders step into their power, make bold decisions, and lead with purpose every day.

Follow Earlene's journey as she continues to make an impact in the fields of media, marketing, leadership, and entrepreneurship.

Connect with Earlene on social media:

Instagram
@earlenecamielle

Facebook
@Earlene Camielle

LinkedIn
@EarleneCamielleCartwright

D.R.E.A.M. in Motion

BY DR. GINA KUHN-ROBATIN

The moment you stepped into leadership—whether by choice or circumstance—you inherited more than just a title. You took on the weight of expectations, the pressure to perform, and the silent question every team member is asking: Can I trust you to lead me? Leadership isn't about power; it's about showing up, owning your influence, and mastering the delicate balance between driving success and fostering a culture where people thrive. But here's the truth no one tells you—most leaders are running on empty, leading from a place of exhaustion rather than inspiration. Sound familiar?

At 33 years old, my life changed in a moment. One minute I was living life as a driven, ambitious woman with big goals and dreams for my future, and the next minute, I was lying in a hospital bed, unable to walk, speak, or move my body in any way. I had a stroke! The stroke didn't just steal my ability to function—it tried to steal my identity, my purpose, and my will to survive.

Even the doctors and nurses had given up hope. They told my husband to bring my boys in and say their goodbyes; I was not going to make it through the night. I must say, hearing your family tell you how much they love you was fuel for my soul. I will never forget that night I lay in the hospital bed, listening to all the machines. I could actually feel every organ in my body begin to fail. My breaths were shallow. My energy was gone. I told myself, *This is it. I'm going to die.*

At that moment, I didn't think about all the arenas I hadn't spoken in yet, the best-selling books I hadn't written, or creating the TV programs to reach the world. No, I thought about the people I loved most and the words I'd never said. I thought about my family and how I'd give anything to simply tell them "I love you" one more time...

And then the morning came.

I woke up. I was alive!

Somehow, despite all odds, I opened my eyes to another day. This was when I fully realized that every moment in life matters. In that instant, I knew I had only two choices: I could lie there and give up and allow my circumstances to define me, or I could fight with everything I had in me.

I decided to fight!

I knew, because of my career as a medical massage therapist for over a decade, that the strongest part of my body was my hands, so I focused all my energy on trying to connect my brain to my hands. I couldn't move anything, but I told myself, *If I could just move my hands, I'd be able to sign "I love you" to my family one more time.* That became my only goal. It wasn't about regaining full control of my whole body yet. It wasn't about reaching a new career goal or speaking in front of large audiences again. It was about one small step that meant the world to me. I wanted my family to know I loved them. They are the breath in my lungs and the reason for my fight.

We all have a story. Maybe yours isn't as dramatic and life-changing as mine; however, you still have a story that has perhaps changed your life in some drastic way. You can choose to allow it to take control and make you stay down, or you can choose to be resilient, find and lean on your inner strength, and get back up again.

The Strength to Lead Starts With a Decision

That moment taught me something profound: True strength doesn't always come from physical ability. It comes from the decisions we make when everything feels impossible. Leadership is no different.

Being a leader doesn't mean having all the answers, being perfect, or even showing vulnerability. It means choosing to show up every day with courage, even when life is hard. It means making the decision to fight for your dreams, your visions, your purpose, and your priorities—even when you don't feel capable.

So many women in leadership feel like they have to do it all and never show weakness. But the truth is, the most successful leaders are the ones who have faced adversity, embraced their imperfections, and risen stronger because of it.

Building a Life That Reflects You

When I eventually regained the ability to move, speak, and live again, I realized that I couldn't go back to the way I had been living before my stroke. My life had to reflect what mattered most to me: my passion, my purpose, and my priorities. A life where my values and success didn't come at the expense of my health, happiness, and relationships. I had to start living as my authentic self in order to enjoy true fulfillment.

You Are Stronger Than You Think

There will be moments in your leadership journey when you feel like giving up; when the weight of expectations, responsibilities, and challenges feels like too much to bear. In those moments, I want you to remember this: You are stronger than you think!

If I could go from lying in a hospital bed, unable to move, to rebuilding my life, then you can overcome whatever challenge you're facing today as well. I believe in you. Strength isn't about having everything figured out; it's about taking the next small step forward, even when the path may not be clear.

Maybe that step is having a difficult conversation with your team. Maybe it's setting boundaries to protect your time and energy. Or maybe it's simply admitting that you're struggling and allowing yourself to ask for help. Whatever your next step is, take it! You don't have to do it all at once; just move forward one step at a time.

The Balance Between Leading and Living

As women, especially those in leadership, we often feel like we have to sacrifice ourselves to succeed. The truth is that leadership and balance are not mutually exclusive. In fact, you cannot be an effective leader if you're constantly burnt out, stressed beyond measure, and disconnected from your authentic self.

How many leaders do you know that can honestly say they are not under tremendous stress and pressure for prolonged periods of time? Did you know that research shows 90% of all illnesses and diseases are caused by stress? Chronic stress has been associated with many kinds of health issues, such as muscle tension, digestive problems, headaches, weight gain, trouble sleeping, heart disease, high blood pressure, and the list goes on.

After hearing this, you must start to wonder how you can meet the demanding business goals and deadlines without sacrificing your values, relationships, or your mental and physical well-being. The answer lies in aligning your leadership with the five-step system I've created for professionals just like you. It's called:

D.R.E.A.M. In Motion

D—Define
R—Refine
E—Engage
A—Align
M—Master

D—Define Your Vision

Every great leader begins with a vision. However, it's not enough to simply have a vision; you must define it with clarity and conviction. A very simple and practical way of thinking about it is like planning to have lasagna for dinner tonight. You first have to decide on lasagna, then you have to reverse engineer it into very specific steps, make a list of all ingredients needed, and then shop to buy them. Continuing on, you must then cook the noodles and the meat separately, layer the pan using all ingredients, and then bake for the allotted time for maximum flavor. Can't you just smell the aroma? It will literally make your mouth water anticipating your first full bite! That is how clear you must have your vision, business plan, and revenue target. It's the big-picture dream that sets your soul on fire. The reason to take on the journey in the first place. Now, envision it in your mind and take the next steps forward.

Start by asking:

- Who is it I want to help?
- What do I want to achieve, and why does it matter?
- How does this vision align with my authentic self?
- What impact do I want to make on my team, my industry, and the world?

Defining your vision is about getting very specific. Write it down and make it clear. Practice visualizing it daily, and share it with your team. The clearer your vision, the more it will inspire action, not just for you but for everyone working alongside you.

R—Refine Your Purpose and Stay Resilient

Once your vision is defined, the next step is to refine your purpose. This is the "Why" behind the "What." Purpose is the fuel that keeps us moving forward, even when challenges arise.

Refining your purpose requires self-reflection and the drive to stay resilient when challenges come. Consider these prompts to help guide you:

- What are my core values, and how do they show up in my leadership?
- How does my purpose align with my team's and my organization's goals?
- Am I pursuing success in a way that feels meaningful and fulfilling?
- How do we refine the mission while staying resilient?

When you refine your purpose, you ensure that every decision you make, both professionally and personally, aligns with what truly matters to you. This alignment creates a ripple effect, empowering those around you to connect with their own purpose and power.

E—Engage Your Power

Authentic leadership is about leading from a place of inner power, not external control. Your power lies in your unique strengths, skills, and experiences. However, the strongest empowerment you need is your mindset, first and foremost. The defeated mindset must go!

To engage that power, you must first own it.

Here's how:

1. **Align your mindset with the direction you want to lead:** Your team must understand the vision to go along with the plan of action.
2. **Acknowledge your strengths:** What do you naturally excel at, and how can you use those skills to lead effectively?
3. **Confront your fears:** Fear of failure or judgment can block your power. What limiting beliefs are holding you

back? How can you change your mindset to reframe them?
4. **Empower others:** True power isn't about being in control; it's about uplifting others. How can you create opportunities for your team to thrive? You'll find that when you give of your time, you will shine!

Engaging your power isn't about striving for perfection; it's about showing up authentically, even in moments of vulnerability. When you lead with honesty and strength, you inspire others to do the same.

A—Align Your Priorities

One of the biggest challenges for leaders is staying focused on what truly matters. Between meetings, deadlines, and endless to-do lists, it's easy to lose sight of your priorities. However, alignment is key to achieving both business success and personal fulfillment.

To align your priorities, start by asking:

- Are my daily actions aligned with my vision and purpose?
- Am I investing my time and energy in tasks that create the most impact?
- How can I delegate or eliminate tasks that don't serve my goals?

Alignment also means setting boundaries. As a leader, it's tempting to say yes to everything, but true alignment requires saying no to distractions and commitments that don't serve your greater vision. Saying no is never easy, but sometimes very necessary to move forward with purpose.

M—Master Your Fulfillment

The final step in the **D.R.E.A.M. In Motion** framework is mastering fulfillment. Success without fulfillment is empty, and yet so many leaders chase external achievement while neglecting their inner well-being.

Mastering fulfillment requires a shift in perspective. Instead of seeing success as an end goal, view it as a journey. Celebrate your wins—big and small. Take time to rest, recharge, and reconnect with what brings you joy.

Here are three practices to help you master fulfillment:

1. **Gratitude:** Start and end each day by reflecting on what you're grateful for. Gratitude shifts your focus from what's missing to what's abundant.
2. **Self-Care:** Prioritize your mental, physical, and emotional health. Start to journal, go for a massage, or go do something fun you've not done in a while. Remember, a fulfilled leader is a resilient leader.
3. **Connection:** Surround yourself with like-minded people who uplift and inspire you both personally and professionally.

When you master fulfillment, you lead from a place of abundance rather than scarcity and a place of joy instead of stress. This not only improves your well-being but also enhances your ability to inspire and motivate others.

One of the greatest joys of being the owner/operator of Dr. Gina's Transformation Academy, LLC, is seeing mindsets shift and dreams come to life. We provide proven systems, courses, and curriculum to help aspiring entrepreneurs and current business owners take a dream they never thought possible and turn it into a thriving reality. So often, I meet women who have incredible ideas but feel stuck, unsure of where to begin, or afraid their vision is too big to achieve. Our mission is to guide them step-by-step, showing them that by using the right system, defining their vision, refining their purpose, and aligning their priorities, anything is possible!

Here are just two of the many success stories given by women we have helped:

Darlene Marie had a passion for horses and a deep connection to the field her family had owned for generations. For years, it was just an open space, but with a bold vision, the right system, and much determination, she turned that field into a multimillion-dollar horse ranch!

When she first started, she didn't believe any of this would be possible. We kept reassuring her she could do it, one step forward at a time. We encouraged her to believe in her strengths, her abilities, and herself. Walking her through the hard times is where she'll tell you she learned to be more resilient than ever. As she stuck to the proven system, allowed drive and determination to keep her going, and envisioned the end goal daily, success was inevitable.

What started as a dream grew into a thriving business that continues to expand year after year. She added an indoor arena and expanded her facilities to board more horses. Her dedication didn't stop there; she went on to train champion horse riders, creating a legacy of excellence.

Pause. I want you to take a minute to reflect.

If we were writing your story, what kind of "champion" do you aspire to be?

Write it out; draw it out in a caricature or an animal. Now I want you to give it a name.

Next, what would be the "legacy of excellence" you would want to leave for your children and family? What would you hope it meant to them? What do you want them to be inspired to do because of it?

I call this "The Ripple Effect" because it has the potential to change your family for generations.

Another story that stands out is Rachel Rose, a stay-at-home mom who always dreamed of owning her own hair salon someday but had no idea where to start. She loved styling hair and longed to build a successful business doing what she loved, but with a busy household and young children, she felt that her dream was out of reach.

One day, Rachel Rose shared her vision with her husband. He could feel her excitement. She was so passionate about her purpose and wanting to use it to help others. They both were on board and together, they got creative. They had decided to transform their garage into a fully functioning, state-of-the-art hair salon. This would allow her the opportunity to work from home while still being present for her children.

This also gave her the flexibility she needed to set her own schedule as much or as little as she wanted while earning a great income doing what she loved. Not only did she create the business she'd always dreamed of, but she also became an example to her children of what is possible when you believe in yourself and take that first step with confidence.

No matter how big or small your dream may seem, it's possible to achieve it with a clear vision and the right system with the keys to success. Whether you want to launch a multimillion-dollar company or start a business that fits seamlessly into your family life, Dr. Gina's Transformation Academy, LLC, is here to help. Let's turn your dreams into reality!

Thank you for investing the time in yourself to read this chapter. My hope is that it has inspired you to put your **D.R.E.A.M. In Motion**. I believe in you. You can do it!

Living your dream as a leader, the ultimate goal is to inspire others while staying true to yourself. The **D.R.E.A.M. In Motion** framework provides a roadmap for achieving this balance:

D—Defining your vision
R—Refining your purpose
E—Engaging your power
A—Aligning your priorities
M—Mastering your fulfillment

And you can achieve business success without losing sight of your authenticity. Authentic leadership and success happen when a company or leader fully integrates the **D.R.E.A.M. In Motion** system, allowing fulfillment into everything they do.

Are you ready to live your dream? If Darlene Marie, Rachel Rose, and I can do it, so can you, my friend! Let's make it happen together. Go to www.drginasacademy.com. Don't let anything stop you from living your authentic self and building the life and business you've always dreamed of.

~

Dr. Gina-Kuhn Robatin is the CEO/Founder of Dr. Gina's Transformation Academy, LLC. She has spent 30 years as an award-winning entrepreneur, keynote speaker, radio personality, female vocalist of the year nominee at Morning Star Records, Nashville, Tennessee, and a published author.

Dr. Gina has traveled to 49 states, captivating audiences and encouraging them to put their **D.R.E.A.M. In Motion**. Her journey from stroke to strength motivated her to thrive as a leader and has shaped her passion for helping women be resilient and empowered—all while finding balance, fulfillment, and success!

Whether you're a CEO or a busy stay-at-home mom, an entrepreneur or looking to start your own business, leadership, purpose, and mindset are the keys to your success, both personally and professionally.

If you're ready to D.R.E.A.M. big, live bold, and embrace your power to create a life you love and enjoy then I invite you to step into your best life with purpose and confidence. It's time to give yourself permission to thrive.

Please visit our website or call Dr. Gina's Transformation Academy, LLC to explore how we can work together to make it happen!

For more information, please visit our website
www.drginasacademy.com

Follow us on:

Facebook
@Gina_KuhnRobatin

LinkedIn
https://www.linkedin.com/in/dr-gina-kuhn-robatin-9814402a7

Lead Within to Lead Beyond

BY HEIDI MECKLEY

Growing up, I was always chosen as a leader. In school, even though I was known as the quiet one, I was often the one to give the answers. Whether punching a clock or working a side hustle, my coworkers considered me a leader in the workplace. But despite this consensus of opinion, I had difficulty seeing myself that way. Back then, I didn't understand what true leadership meant. I have a much better understanding now.

As a child, I was afraid of being seen. I didn't want anyone to know about all the crazy things going on at home. I didn't want people relying on me because I knew I was going to leave as soon as I could. Three days after graduation, I moved out.

Even though things were rough in my personal life, I always found my way through. There were times I was home alone for weeks or even months, yet I would get up and go to school, come home and do my homework, and do everything that was necessary to take care of myself. I saw school as a safe place; it got me away from home, and I knew I needed a diploma to make something of myself. I decided I wanted to be the type of person who works to finish things, not leave them hanging. I chose to control the things I could. I kept on being who I chose to be.

Fast forward to October 2019. That was a day that changed everything for me. I had a nasty fall on the landing at the top of the stairs, hitting my head and shoulder as I went down and landing hard on my hip. My shoulder required surgery for a rotator cuff tear, and I had a severe concussion. For the next two and a half years, I would experience post-concussion syndrome (PCS). I had trouble walking, talking, and taking care of my basic needs. A part of me wanted to give up and accept this as my new normal. But an even bigger part of me refused to accept it. "NO!" I said, "I *will* find my way back."

So I did just that.

Now, when people ask what I would change in my life, the answer is and will always be the same: NOTHING! Why do I say that? If I changed one second of my past, I would not be who I am today, surrounded by the people I am with, and doing what I do. I regret nothing; every bit of it was a lesson learned that I can now pass on to those who come into my world. This has become both my passion and my mission: to help others understand that they are not alone and can succeed regardless of what they have been through.

My Fall and Recovery

The day of the fall, I felt like I had it all together. We were clearing the yard of some trees that fell from a storm. I had a beauty business at the time (this was before launching my coaching/mentoring business). I had been running around doing all the things. Life seemed great, yet I felt like something was missing. The fall allowed me to see that I was doing things simply because I thought they were what I should be doing. What you *should* do, what is *right* to do, and what you *get* to do are all very different things. When you are doing things only because you or someone else thinks you should, you will always feel like something is missing. Doing what is right will fuel your purpose and help you see that you can make things happen. But the best part is when you can say, *I get to do this*. That is when you are living your life on your terms.

I fell in October, and I had vendor events set up with the beauty business all the way through January. They were all paid, so if I did not attend, I would lose the funds. With the help of my amazing husband and son, we made them happen; ironically, the worst year for my health was one of my best sales years. I realized that because there were so many things I couldn't do, it gave me the time to focus on the one thing that brought in the funds: my beauty biz. So many times, I felt guilty for asking my husband and son to help. However, they were always there whenever I needed them. I do not remember a lot from that time frame—it's all a blur—but I have realized that I needed that to get me on my true track and purpose in life. I am here to help others in a monumental way, and although helping people to have amazing skin and getting them to look their best is good; guiding people to their purpose and working with them on a strategy to have a successful business and/or life has so much more meaning behind it.

I still have issues with PCS to this day. I am not sure I will ever be 100% back to where I was, and that is okay. I don't need to get lost in doing things just to be doing something when there is a much higher calling in my life. It took me until I was 47 to realize that I needed to look within. I had to be okay with others talking about me because I could not do everything I did before or help in the ways I used to. This happened during the COVID pandemic, and I hid in the house for those years. I had to drive over an hour one way to go to a concussion clinic for help, but after 10 minutes, I'd be extremely dizzy with massive pressure in my head. You cannot see the effects of a concussion, so people didn't realize the issues I was facing.

Most of the time, I was home alone; my husband was at work, and my son was at school. I could have easily given up and just allowed this to be my new normal. But I have always been driven to make things happen, and I knew that wasn't the life I wanted. When I noticed thoughts of giving up, I would say, *No, I am stronger than this. I know I was made for more.* I reminded myself that this fall had happened to allow me to better align with what my purpose here on this planet would be.

Since I was not able to do much, I knew the one thing I could and should be doing was working on myself. I joined a major player in the coaching industry and started a journey to learn and grow. I don't recall much from those first couple of years, but I somehow fully knew the fall was a way to get my attention. Each time I felt myself pulled in a direction, I started taking action. I wrote my first book only three months after launching my coaching business. I had to realize that I have control of what is going on in my head and that I am the only one who can do anything about it. I had to look at what I was going through and see it as a way to get on my path and find my purpose. That purpose is to guide others to connect with their own soul's purpose, along with the actions needed to make that purpose work for them.

Are you someone who has big dreams and goals, yet you don't feel empowered to make them happen? Or maybe you are determined but feel like you're spinning your wheels? Are you struggling to find purpose or meaning in life? My aim is to help you reach your goals and achieve your dreams, then create new ones and do it all again.

My hope for you in reading this chapter is for you to learn to be open—to look deep within yourself, at a deeper level than just the surface, and find out what you are really here for—so that you can learn to plan and create the life that most people only dream of. So when it is your time to go, you will not be sad, regretful, or remorseful. Instead, when you live your life without regret, you will feel blessed, fulfilled, and grateful for the amazing life you chose to live on your terms.

Lead Yourself Before You Can Lead Others

So, how do you make all that happen? First, you need to understand what it means to *lead yourself before you can lead others*. Resist the temptation to guide others through their issues before you deal with your own. To be the best leader you can be, you have to walk the talk. This means you must not tell *anyone* to do *anything* you have not done yourself. This isn't always easy. Every parent can think of a time when they told their child what not to do and then did it themselves. By leading yourself first, you will gain respect from others. In order to develop the self-awareness this requires, you need to be fully connected to your soul and its purpose.

How does leading yourself have a ripple effect on all those around you? Look at it this way: Those who have good things going on in their lives always have people around them who want to know how they are doing it. Some will truly want to learn what you are doing so they can level up—that is a close ripple. Then, people around them will ask them what they have been doing, and will want to learn about it—that is a second ripple, and so on down the line. At first, you may only have a couple of people show interest, but once you and others show the changes in your lives—how happy you are and all you can do with your time—more will be asking how to get the lifestyle you have. It isn't for us to keep to ourselves; it is for us to share and teach others to get there.

Lead With Your Soul's Purpose

Everyone I have spoken to over the years desires an authentic connection to themselves and their purpose. However, they don't know how to see it, feel it, or get it. I fully understand this, as I have been there.

When I fell, I was 47, divorced, remarried to my junior high sweetheart, and wondering what I was supposed to be doing. I was happy, and I could make a lot happen in a day. However, most of it didn't have any meaning behind it. It was like going through the motions at a rapid pace. I wasn't being fulfilled. I wasn't finding my joy and peace, something we all are searching for. I wanted to know what I was here for and wondered if I was doing the things that aligned with my purpose.

In life, we often take on other people's expectations for us as if they were ours to carry. We let their fears and worries block us from doing the things we dream of or want to accomplish. You have to ask yourself if what you are doing is only because others thought you should. Is it simply because you are good at it? Or are you doing it because it lights you up and you have an unending passion for it?

Once I started looking inward, I realized I was blessed with the gift of being able to help others see, understand, and work to correct the things that are blocking them from their true purpose and a life beyond what they could imagine. *That* was my passion. It took a nasty fall for me to see that everything else I was doing was just busy work; it would never get me to a place to help thousands over my lifetime, and that was my mission and purpose.

Stay true to who you are and your purpose; don't let the shiny things take you off track. Once you truly lock in your purpose, you can finally start taking the intentional steps needed to make your dreams and goals a reality.

Aligning with your purpose is extremely empowering. You will see what the issues are and the next steps you need to take. You may not get the entire path, but that will come in time. Learn to lean into this and not be so stressed when you don't see everything at once. We are not always meant to see the whole picture because things change along the path, which means the goal or dream can change as well. When you find your goals and dreams changing along the way, it means you were meant for something bigger than you originally set out for.

Learning to live on your terms, your path, and in alignment with your soul gives you the life you are wishing for. The question is: Are you really willing to do the work to get there?

Start Small—But Get Started!

As we go through life, we change, and our desires will evolve, too. In order to find your passion, you have to start by taking small steps. Create a small goal, and take the steps needed to achieve it. Once you prove to yourself that you *can* accomplish your goals, dream bigger, then make it happen! You will find that these small successes ignite a passion within you and guide you to your mission—the reason you are here. Once you truly understand your mission, you will go to the ends of the earth to bring it to fruition. Ask yourself, *What dream or idea do I still have that I have not taken action on yet?* Then make the decision to do so. I know most of you are thinking, *I don't know where to start or how to make it happen.* Guess what? That is how every great invention or idea started. The difference between making it happen and staying stuck is *action*. What one small thing will start you on your journey to make it happen right now? *You* are the one who has to start. It is *your* dream or goal—no one else's—so why do you keep asking everyone what they think? Embrace your free will. We all have the desire to go after things in our lives, but it is up to us to take action and make them happen. No one else is going to do it for you. So what are you waiting for?

Avoid Overthinking

My work often requires me to guide my clients to see that the truth is usually not as bad as they are making it out to be. When we overthink, we make things so much worse in our heads than what is really going on. Believe me, I used to do it as well. I was an avid overthinker, working to see all the angles of the negative things that could happen. Now, I see it for what it is and do not allow it to take the time or energy it does not deserve. Our minds can make something so much worse or so much better than it is. When you learn to be *soul-aligned*, you become continuously aware of what you are doing and thinking so you can correct your course as needed. You will then feel so much more in control and have a better understanding of what is happening at the moment instead of sitting on it and stewing over it, making it worse, taking your energy, and more.

Once you start on this path, you start showing up differently—more focused, more driven, and more committed to what you are going after. Isn't this exactly what we are looking to have?

Learn to Look Inward

I have been in some form of direct sales business since I was 19. I am so grateful for those years; I learned so much from all those people. I had many fears and did not believe I could do something like that and not need a "real job." Everyone in the businesses wanted me to shoot to hit $10k/month, but people around me kept telling me there was no way I would ever make anything with those businesses. Remember, you are the sum of the five people you are closest to. For me, at the time, those people wanted to hold me back, but I did not realize that's what they were doing.

How many times have you thought about going after a goal, told people about it, and they shut you down? Or how many times have you tried to go after goals that others tell you that you should go after, but you never reach them? How did either of these make you feel? Many people feel pressured to move as fast as they can and do as much as they can, but for what? We miss out on life when we are trying to make everyone else happy or do work that is not aligned with our path.

We know that other people's expectations, fears, or just past experiences can create blocks that stop us from living the life we were designed to. We take what they say as true, yet it does not align with who we are or our purpose. Sometimes, we let others' negativity shut us down. Sometimes, we self-sabotage. As adults, we need to start figuring out who we are and what we want to do with our lives. We have all been asked the question since we were kids, and you may have answered using all the stories, expectations, and fears that you picked up from other people early in life. You must take everything you've learned and decide what you want to keep and what you want to get rid of. It is your life, your mind, and your soul. You are its keeper and nurturer—no one else. Carrying around bits and pieces of everyone else's life does not give you space to be you. You need to remember the dreams you have are yours, no one else's. It is up to you to work through them and believe in them. Yes, you can ask others for help to get to where you want to go, as we do not get there alone. However, if they are telling you that your dream is crazy or not working, then those are not the people who can help you.

Once you strip back all the things inside that are not you and understand who you truly are, you will be able to make your own authentic decisions based on your purpose. When stripped clean of everyone's expectations, thoughts, and fears, you can see and feel what you want and who you are. It is basically stripping away all the expectations of the world to just be you. It's something so many search for, yet never find.

If you keep allowing others to tell you how to live your life, you will never get to where *you* want to go. Your dreams and goals are yours, not theirs. Few will understand the drive you have to go after that goal; you need to chase your dreams regardless. It may be hard at first, but once you start making traction, everything will fall into place. You'll have the opportunity to prove to yourself that you've got this. Because God, the Universe, Source, or whatever you want to call it, gave it to you for a reason. This world needs what you are going after.

Once you are fully *soul-connected* and aligned with yourself and your goals, the expectations of those around you will not bother you; nothing will stop you from pursuing your dreams and goals. You'll no longer feel the need to explain your desire to anyone because you won't need anyone's approval.

Use the following steps to take action now:

Step One: Find Clarity

One key piece to all of this is *clarity!* Without clarity, you will always struggle and be frustrated. Looking within and doing the real work to strip away the things that are not you is a must to have a life others only dream about. Most often, you will need the assistance of a guide or coach to help you find clarity.

Step Two: Write it Out

What does it mean to look inward? It means you have to do the real work on *you*. Allow yourself to be the person you are meant to be; let go of the stories, fears, and things from your past or that others placed in your mind. It's not difficult; it is work, however.

Start with the understanding that your mind is going to fight you because you are doing something different. However, here is a secret: It is *your* mind, and *you* are in control of it. No one else. Just like with anything else, it will take a bit of time to declutter and prove to your mind that you are in control and not your subconscious.

I am betting you are asking yourself, *Well, how the heck do I do that?* Well... the next step—the one that will keep you in control of what you are doing and more—is to journal. I know you have heard this before, but you haven't fully committed yet. Maybe you start and stop or have trouble when you sit to write. Well, this is the secret sauce to making massive changes in your mind and life. It truly is amazing what happens when you put pen to paper. Try it! You will not regret it.

It does not need to be neat, organized, or structured to get started. You need to find what works best for you. I also *highly* recommend having two journals. Here is why: There are going to be times when you are having a rough go, and you will write thoughts that you may not want anyone else to see. I call this one the WTF journal. (Make this one a cheap one, because you are writing things that will cause you stress if others get their hands on it.) Then you need to rip out the pages and burn them after writing them. When you do burn them, say the following as it is burning: *I release all the negative thoughts on these pages and release them to you (God, the Universe, Source, or whatever you feel comfortable saying). I no longer align with those thoughts, and I am choosing to work to be my highest self.*

The first few times you do this, you should then write in the other journal the feelings and emotions you went through during the process of releasing all those thoughts. Journaling allows you to truly observe your patterns, blocks, and excuses from your own words. How amazing is that?

Look back every few days and read what you wrote. Be objective; you may even want to pretend someone else wrote it so you can see the patterns, issues, or wins much faster. Then, do your writing for that day. Journaling is truly a daily task that everyone should incorporate into their daily to-dos. Please know it is okay if this takes you a bit of time to get down. Understanding your deep-rooted limiting beliefs, blocks, and excuses is a journey, so you will have to work to make this a daily habit. Put it all out there. Use this prompt to go deeper: *Why am I doing what I am doing?* You will have to answer this a few times in order to get the real answer. Answering this one time will only give you the surface answer. Go deeper! You may need to do this seven to ten times. Keep asking "Why" for each answer until you get the deepest meaning of what you are going after.

Once you understand exactly why you are going for what you are after, find someone to teach you how to do that thing and go all in. Learn it like your life depended on it, and pay attention to how you feel, what you are doing differently, and so on. Work to find like-minded people to surround yourself with that will lift you up when it gets bumpy, because it will get bumpy. It is all in how you handle it and see it as to how fast you can smooth out those bumps. And if you have trouble making the connections or seeing the patterns because you are too close to them, this is where a great guide/coach/mentor can come in to help you see, embrace, and show up as the person you are meant to be.

Step Three: Avoid Overwhelm

Once you get into your purpose, it is so easy to wear yourself out because you just want to go after it. It is fantastic that you have dialed in, but you still need to be present for your needs and those of the people you care for.

On your path, you're going to encounter times of difficulty. What do you do when you feel overwhelmed? I have a foolproof way to get you out of it fast. Try this the very next time you are feeling overwhelmed:

> *The first thing you need to do is to stop and catch yourself in the midst of overwhelm. Yes, you can do this, and it isn't as hard as you might think. Next, grab a pen and paper and write out all the things that are causing you to feel overwhelmed. Now sit and really look at the list with new eyes. Stop stressing over things that you cannot control. Remember that you are in charge of your feelings. Think about your purpose, and you will realize that there is no need to allow these things to make you feel this way.*

Step Four: Take Action

Finally, take one action step to address one of the items on your list. By doing this, you take back your power; you will find yourself shifting from negative to positive thinking by taking control of both your thoughts and actions. Action is always the key to getting out of negative thoughts.

I dare you to try this. (And if you post about how well it worked, tag me @heidimeckley and use #hmcoverwhelmhack so I can cheer you on!)

You've got this; I believe in you! Don't give up! Your life is so worth it, and we need what you were put here to do. And always, always make sure you are taking time away from your dream to take care of you!

Setting Goals

Once you have started breaking through and seeing what the underlying issues are, you are ready to start working towards being *soul-aligned* with your goals. What does that mean? Being *soul-aligned* with your goals is where the magic happens; it means you are truly going after things that are connected with your soul's purpose!

However, you have to do the journaling work to get to this point. If you do not work to get out all the thoughts, ideas, and rules of others in your life to create what is truly aligned with you, who you are, and your purpose, you will only get frustrated with not hitting the goals you want.

Once you get to this point, your goals are going to be *soul-connected*. These are the goals you will not give up on; they are the ones you will keep working on until you get there or a bigger and better goal takes their place.

To better explain this, I would like to give you a couple of examples. Many people who are working for themselves pick a number or dollar amount to shoot for. Suppose you are working to make $10k a month by June. This goal is money-driven without spelling out *why* you want it. If you are picking that dollar amount because a coach or someone in your industry said to, it's someone else's goal, not yours. It is not *soul-aligned;* there is no real meaning behind it. You may think you want it, but as soon as you say it, do you hear negative thoughts like, *How the heck can I do that when I can barely make $2k a month?* Or *I can't hit that goal!* If so, you'll start thinking about all the other goals you haven't reached, which makes you feel like a failure. You will have feelings come up from your past that hold you back and prevent you from doing what you know you need to do to achieve this goal.

Now, say you have been journaling and doing the inner work. Rather than starting with a money goal, think deeper. If you want to earn $10k a month, reverse engineer that goal by figuring out *exactly* what you need to do to get there. If your mission is to help others, think about how many people you will need to help to earn $10k. Then, create your goal from there: *My goal is to help 25 people this month.* Just saying you want to hit a dollar amount won't get you there. When you connect your goal with your purpose, it becomes your mission, and you are fully *soul-connected* to it. By getting to the meaning that pulls at your heartstrings, you will find ways to keep going after what you want, regardless of the roadblocks that pop up in your path. I mean, stop for a second and really think about all the things you have given up on in your life. If you are reading this book, it means you want to change that and not only make your mark but also have a life that is full of joy, peace, and success.

Let me give you a couple of personal examples of getting connected and making goals happen. In 2019, my husband and I decided that we didn't want to stay in one place; we wanted to travel. Now we had our kiddo, so we knew we would need to press pause until he graduated from high school, and that was okay. That time would allow us to start lining things up and getting our mindsets ready for the huge jump. See, we live in our (okay, my) dream home. A home that is very unique and large—2600 sq. ft. on just under two acres on a dead-end road.

From that summer in 2019, we would look at RVs online and in person and attend RV events. We had to explain to our son that we were not doing this to make him feel like we wanted him out of the house, just that when you have a huge dream like we had, you have to keep thinking about it and making decisions, keeping your dream in mind to make it happen. I have come up with a very specific way to make goals a reality by writing them down (there's a bit more to it, but we'll get to that). We were talking about and looking at so many RVs that it could get confusing. However, we had to figure out what type of layout we would be happy with. I mean, we were going to live in it after all; we'd need to be comfortable.

Fast forward to March 13, 2024. I decided to start adding the RV to my goal list that I wrote out daily. I wrote, "We have found our perfect starter RV." The next day, I was thinking, *This doesn't feel right. I don't want a starter. I want what I want—a high-end, well-made, and known-to-last RV.* So I changed it to, "We found the perfect RV for us." Fast forward to October 2024, and I changed it again: "We found the perfect RV for us at an amazing price." Of course, the ones I really wanted were outside our budget for sure—well over six figures. On December 3, 2024, we signed the papers for the brand and model of the RV I had been drooling over for less than six figures! It took nine months to bring that dream to life.

When a salesperson asks if they can help you find something, have you ever responded with "I'll know it when I see it?" I bet most of you are nodding your head yes. Now let me ask you, how would it feel to say that about all your huge goals? To know it when you see it. That is what it means to be *soul-aligned;* you won't settle for anything other than what you are after. Does this mean you are never frustrated? NO, it is life, after all. You will still get frustrated and have bad days. But now you have the understanding that you have the control to bring it back to the positive. The things you are going through are truly helping you to learn what you need for the next level up in life. You need to prove to yourself that you are after what your soul is aligned with. When that happens, you won't stop until you get it, and when everything hits the fan, you'll see it as a test. Then you will need to ask yourself *How much do you want what is on the other side of the issues?* Trust me, I know what it is like when life derails you. However, I have found that with understanding, you can breeze right through.

Success Stories

I had a client who was always overwhelmed and felt very frustrated. Although she was sort of organized, she felt very disorganized. She had issues with setting and writing out goals. She had relationship issues from what happened in her past and so much more. She was working in a direct sales company, and still is, that she really believed in, but was not really making the sales quotas she had to reach the income she really needed. Together, we realized that although she loved this company, her heart was pointing her in a different direction. First, we worked together for several months, going deep to pull the weeds of what she was allowing to hold her back. She was very grateful when her relationships improved once she was able to see them in a new light. We then did a one-off session on setting goals and how to go after them. She would write out the goals for her business based on what those in her upline were saying she should be shooting for. Okay, hands up or nod if you have been here before. As we had done a lot of the deeper work already, I was quickly able to show her she was shooting for surface-level goals, but more importantly, goals that were not hers. Once you get in alignment with what you are doing in life and business and are going after your purpose, your goal writing is much deeper and connected, which means you will do whatever it takes to make it happen. She was so excited to finally understand and be able to really take action on what she wanted out of life that she even did a live video in my group about it. She was that dream client that everyone wants—a person who listens and then takes action on what they learn.

I had a couple of other clients who, during the initial calls, stated they had issues with their mothers, but that wasn't what was holding them back. In the end, we found for both that, in fact, that was exactly what was holding them back. By working intuitively, I was able to walk them both through why it was their issue, and then how they could work to take their power back to live a life they want, not what their mothers wanted or felt they should be doing.

All my clients have had amazing breakthroughs and understandings of what they were allowing to hold them back from the life of their dreams. We worked together to pull those weeds so they could live their lives as they chose, not by the stories, expectations, and traumas that they had allowed to control their lives.

The one male client I had was one of the toughest to get to journal, as I am sure you can all understand. Most men do not like to talk about how they feel, let alone write it out! At every meeting, I would ask if he had done any writing yet. The answer would always be, "No, but I have it in my head. I know what it is." Each time I would explain that keeping it in his head is only making things worse, and he needs to get it out to see what is really happening. Unless you have done this type of work, it is hard to understand the outcome and how much better you feel. We missed a meeting, and at the very next one, he stated that he sat down and wrote things out. He was amazed at not only how much better he felt but how much he wrote—five pages front and back! As he read over what he had written, he was able to find some issues in his thinking and, in turn, his actions. Taking that time to let it out on paper and just release it was a massive breakthrough for him, and now he had this tool to help him for the rest of his life.

Now Is The Time

Remember, in order to be a great leader, you must fully learn to lead yourself by walking the walk, talking the talk, and doing the do. Once you do the inner work, you will have the tools you need for any obstacle you face because look at all you uncovered, released, and have gone through. If you can do that, you can make it through anything life gives you. Just remember that all those obstacles and setbacks are tests to make sure you are ready for what comes next. Only you can decide if you really want a different life. Only you can decide if the pull is strong enough to become the leader you were destined for.

Start journaling. Start noticing how you are thinking, speaking, and reacting to things. Does it align with the leader you know you are? If not, you just found the most important piece, the trigger to your profound transformation. Because once you see where the issues are, then you can correct them to align with the life you are after!

When you are ready to take the next steps, I would love to invite you to join me in a group program (**Rise to Greatness or Accountability In Action**) or a one-on-one program (**Ignite Your Empire**). Let's work to uncover your soul's purpose, create a strategy for success, and help you lead yourself and others into a life of true fulfillment. Not sure which program is right for you? Reach out and request a coffee chat to my email at heidimeckleycoaching@gmail.com. Or connect with me on LinkedIn : Heidi Meckley Soul-Aligned Success Coach | LinkedIn, follow on Facebook or TikTok. I am easily found under my name. You can also grab my eBook, which is free, on LinkedIn as well.

Now it's your turn to rise to your greatness!

Heidi Meckley is a no-BS soul healer, business mentor, and psychic medium on a mission to help women conquer self-doubt, reclaim their power, and build unstoppable lives. She's the go-to coach for action-takers who are ready to break free from excuses, embrace their soul's purpose, and create a business (and life) that actually lights them up. A published author and sought-after speaker, Heidi blends deep soul work with straight-talk strategy, making transformation feel not just possible but inevitable.

When she's not coaching powerhouse women, you'll find her traveling the country with her husband, coffee in hand, meeting incredible souls, and proving that living your dream life isn't just for other people—it's for you, too.

Book a Call

Find Heidi at: www.heidimeckley.com

Facebook
Heidi Meckley

LinkedIn
Heidi Meckley Soul-Aligned Success Coach

Free eBook
The Power Of Choices

Branding With Soul, Leading With Impact

BY KATIE SMETHERMAN HOLMES

My name is Katie Smetherman Holmes, and I am obsessed with art and design. I am the founder and CEO of the Brand Studio Creative design agency, and I love working with clients who are ready to stop struggling with their brand and start thriving. For more than ten years, I have been able to help clients scale their business with effective brand strategy and website design. I am an avid reader of fantasy books, a dog mom, a baker, a gardener, and a video game nerd.

Throughout my childhood, I was surrounded by creativity, compassion, and heart. I was fortunate to be surrounded by strong women in my family that helped guide me in these beliefs as I grew up. My mother was passionate about being creative and encouraged me early on to explore my creativity. She loved gardening, painting, and cooking. I learned so much from my mother that I appreciate and carry with me to this day. My godmother helped me find my true calling and passion when I was studying for my undergraduate degree and struggling to pick my major. Without these two strong women in my life, I wouldn't be who I am today.

This chapter is for business leaders who are ready to step into their softer side and grow to be heart-centered leaders in today's business world. Gone are the days where business growth was only dictated by financial numbers. It is time to connect with your clients on an emotional level and grow together. Leading with heart and empathy is not a weakness but a strength, especially when it comes to business leadership and connecting with your clients.

With over ten years of experience in design and marketing, I bring expertise in brand identity systems, brand strategy, and website design and development. I have helped clients in over 25 different industries, providing fresh branding perspectives and targeting their unique business goals to help clients get out of stress and into growth.

In my free time, I am an avid reader, but in my business time, I am an avid researcher. I love learning about my clients' niches and will deep dive into researching their industries and best practices to help them grow and succeed. Learning new, exciting ways in design and business development is one of the many skills I bring to the table when I work with clients.

My readers will learn how to tap into their emotional side and use that as a strength in building their connection with their clients and partners. They will become stronger business leaders not only for their internal employees but outward as well with their partners and clients.

I hope that by integrating these five key elements within your business practices, you will not only build deeper business relationships but also grow together with your community and network. The world is looking for authentic people who will not see them just as another number in their business books but as someone they can rely on and trust with their business challenges and struggles.

Leading With Heart

Throughout my life, I have always been told, "You have big emotions." Most of the time, it was said in a derogatory tone to try and put me down or belittle me. However, as I have grown into an adult, I have realized that having "big emotions" and being able to tap into my softer side was so much more of a strength than a weakness. I began noticing that when my friends were struggling with the stresses of everyday life, they would often turn to me for comfort and advice. I never minded this since I have always enjoyed helping others get out of their dark place and into the light. Little did they know, having persistent depression and anxiety gives me a unique advantage in navigating the dark and how to get out of it.

With every client, every network connection, and every new face that enters my life, I always lead with heart. Many find this surprising, especially in business, where so many people are conditioned to keep their emotions in check and only be serious during business hours. However, the more I interact and learn about people, the more I realize that you cannot take the heart out of the business when your business revolves around people. People are the heart of your business, so why remove the piece that makes us human and only see them as a number? Now, am I meaning for you to be a complete mess and share all the chaotic parts of your personal life with your clients? No. That would be madness. However, if you find ways to connect with your clients as people and get on their level, then the connection that you will forge is that much stronger.

Life is messy. And running a business only adds to the mess. But one thing is consistent: people. People want to buy from real, authentic people. We are programmed as humans to want to find a connection with those around us. So why not bring that into your business? Why not bring more of your heart, your passions, and your dreams into your business? I have found that the more I authentically connect with my clients, the more my clients trust me and become returning clients. I never boast or expect loyalty from my clients. I don't believe in that kind of mindset. I do believe in my clients and the amazing things they accomplish. I also believe that good design can change the world, and a lot of the time, it begins with the heart.

Build Authentic Connections

Naivete is an unfortunate side effect when you are first stepping into your career. It's something that a lot of us go through but never really talk about in a "learning experience" kind of way. Many of us acknowledge that it happened and then quickly shove it in a box in our mind and put it in the very back of our brain, never to be seen from or heard from again. However, this is not a very healthy way of processing the experience, according to my therapist, who has a long list of credentials and helpful coping mechanisms that have not only transformed me as a person but also how I connect with others.

So, jumping right into one of my naive moments so that you may also learn from my experience, I want you to step into my shoes as I was fresh out of college and ready to join the American working class. I had just graduated and was going on many interviews without much luck—despite my talents—when I received an offer at a small start-up company. I decided to take the job to gather more experience in the real world of design and marketing. The owner was quite eccentric, and we didn't always see eye to eye, but the team members beside me were fantastic people with similar work ethics, passions, and hearts to mine. I worked closely with the creative director, and we became fast friends and remain friends to this day. Soon after, I was given many tasks that would have been assigned to a senior designer even though I was still at the entry level. Being a fast learner, I learned how to do many jobs and tasks efficiently without sacrificing high-quality design in order to help our clients grow in their businesses.

Despite the pros of the job, some cons were revealed the longer we worked at the company. The team members soon learned about certain financial troubles and incorrect investment handling that were not morally or ethically okay. Soon after learning this information, many of the team members, including myself, left the company to find other jobs. This was a hard adult life lesson that honestly kicked my butt, especially so soon after graduating.

Not every connection is going to be a perfect fit. You may not even realize it until you have collaborated for a while, but that doesn't mean that you need to stay with the relationship just because of time accrued together. You have permission to walk away from a relationship, personal or business, if it doesn't align with your morals and values. For me, that was a hard lesson to learn, especially since growing up I loved being able to be of service and help those around me. Humans are complex creatures with different views and goals. Learning how to be authentic and transparent with your network helps you find people who connect with you.

Since learning how to be more in tune with my gut and allowing myself to leave a connection if I don't see it fitting, I now fully lead with authenticity and transparency with all my network connections. People are built differently, and with that, people connect with people in various ways. I use this to not only find people who I share similar values with, but also encourage me to grow as well. Now, whenever I have my client intake calls, I make sure there is open dialogue not only about the project but also the goals, struggles, and challenges they wish to overcome. If I don't feel like I am a right fit, I am open with them or refer them to one of my network of people.

Empathy Is Empowering

Why does picking out a major always have to be one of the most stressful and hardest things in life? Or why does it seem that way whenever you are in the thick of college?

Now, is it actually the hardest thing in life? No. But society loves to put that pressure on us when we are young. I was deep into my college undergrad, and I felt like I was failing at life because I couldn't pick a major that I was passionate about. I went to my godmother's house, all in a huff of stress and tears, telling her that my life had no direction and I was about to give up on choosing a career path. Little did I know that this moment would be one of the most defining moments of my life.

I walked into my godmother's house, which was always a blend of sarcasm and cozy atmosphere, two of my favorite things. My godmother was married with three beautiful children, and I would spend many summers and weekends hanging out and swimming in their pool. Her husband is a perfumer, and she used to be a salesperson. Both are charismatic in their own way and best friends since college and have a very sarcastic sense of humor that I love. Her husband would go to work every day doing something he was passionate about and come home still full of energy. I always admired that about him and wondered what his secret was.

While sitting on one of the cozy couches, wrapped in a fuzzy blanket, even though it was the dead of summer—but hey, we live in Texas so we have AC blasting all the time—my godmother gave me my space to be authentic. My godmother sat and listened to me rant and vent about how I had no passions and would never find a career with anything that I liked because nothing excited me. All of it was completely untrue, but she sat there and listened for hours. Never once did she call me a liar or interrupt me or tell me "everything will be okay"—which no one actually believes at the moment anyway. Finally, when she felt like I had exhausted myself, she said, "Let me help you. I know if we put our brains together, we can find something you are passionate about just like my husband is about his job." She pulled up her little laptop and began typing away. I would say half sentences, and she would listen and type away on her computer. I felt like I was talking gibberish at her, but she never looked at me like I was crazy or dumb; she just actively listened. She listened between the lines.

"What about graphic design?" She said as my face was deep in a pillow.

To which I simply responded, "What is that?"

We then deep-dived into learning about graphic design and found that my current school had a top-rated program. I fell in love. Well, as in love as you can be with an idea. Sixteen years later, and I am still as passionate about graphic design as I was when I was looking at my godmother's little laptop. She gave me a safe space to find my true self, and now I carry that safe space for all my clients. All of my clients go through a similar process. I listen to their struggles, challenges, goals, and dreams, and then, after I feel like they have said their piece, I share ways on how I can help alleviate those struggles and achieve those goals.

Listen With Compassion

Not to brag or anything, but having persistent depression does come with some perks. Would I recommend it to a friend? No, because depression sucks. But it has taught me how to sit in the mud with anyone.

Living with depression has also given me a unique outside perspective. Hear me out on this one. In layman's terms, depression is one of those fun mental illnesses that sucks the joy out of life. And by fun, I mean not fun at all. I have spent many sleepless nights trapped with my own personal demons, trying to unravel the issues in my brain and mask my internal feelings from the world. I learned that this is not healthy, according to my therapist. It did, however, help me to understand a lot of what many others in the world are struggling with, which made me feel more confident about being able to help others.

I never want to be on a pedestal or placed above others that I am collaborating with. Being very introverted, I typically shy away from the spotlight, though I have gained more confidence in how to navigate that world. But in truth, I would much rather sit side by side, in the thick of the mud, as someone is trying to navigate their brand and give their concerns an area to breathe. So often, I feel that people navigating their business for the first time think that they need to keep their negative thoughts and demons buried deep below. But in reality, those demons and struggling thoughts need a safe space to breathe. Let them out in the open, be honest about them, and then it's so much easier to find little ways to fix or change your perspective.

Compassion is such a powerful way to connect with others and is crucial in leadership. Compassion takes the heart of empathy and creates a tangible experience for you to relate to and help those in need.

Don't Be Afraid to Play

Remember when you were a kid, and all you wanted to do was play? Why did you ever stop once you became an adult? I never understood how, when you grow up, so many people expect you to stop playing and only focus on serious things.

I was fortunate enough to grow up with a mom who loved being creative. When she was creating, she was playing. Whether it was cooking for her family and friends, painting the latest woodworking piece my dad built, or tending to her garden, she always found ways to bring her joy by playing. Even when we would have family and friends over, she would think of fun conversation topics or things for everyone to play together.

I was not as extroverted as my mother was, but I did enjoy creating something from nothing. I would draw, paint, sculpt, write, bake, game, puzzle, and read—anything that would keep me active in creating. Whenever I was in my creative mode, I felt I was being my most authentic self. Even in low times, if I was creating, I still felt like *me*.

As I continued to grow up, I saw how hard adulting can be and would see the stress in my friends and family as well. I began to ask my friends when was the last time they did something just for fun. When was the last time they played? For most of them, life just got too busy. It's super easy to fall prey to imposter syndrome with how many social media platforms are out there and with everyone always posting their best of the best. But everyone is always dealing with something behind closed doors. Everyone is human, and we all are living this life for the first time. It's time to give yourself a break and go play. Whatever it is that brings you joy and fun, of course, without being hard on yourself or others, get out there and go do it. When was the last time you gave yourself permission to play?

Serve to Empower

Serving others was a value drilled into me throughout my childhood. It didn't matter if it was a family member, an adult, or someone I had just met. You are meant to do more than serve yourself; you must also serve others. My mother would berate me if a family member asked for my help, and I didn't respond with "Yes, of course" or "How may I help you?"

When I was a young girl, my mother and I were part of a philanthropy organization for mothers and daughters from middle school through high school. You could join your city's chapter, or a community chapter if you lived in a larger city, and do volunteer work in your local community. This could include anything from walking dogs at a local shelter to stocking food banks with community donations or assisting nonprofits with simple office tasks. By the way, these were all volunteer projects that I worked on during my time with the organization. My favorite, of course, was walking the dogs. I even convinced one of my childhood friends to join me. It had just rained and was so muddy, but we walked dogs through the mud behind the building, getting coated in dirt by the end of the day. We laughed so much that day with each dog that we walked as they ran and dragged us through the mud. Meanwhile, my mom was inside repairing broken dog toys and stitching them back up.

I loved doing philanthropy work. I loved being able to help people in areas where extra hands were needed and seeing the joy that it brought them. This volunteer work continued to inspire us to stay within the program. During the final year, you begin working on your senior presentation, which is kind of like a coming-out for debutantes but without all the showmanship. That year turned out to be the most challenging. Many of our chapter's girls and mothers became so caught up with all the pageantry of the presentation that they forgot we were a philanthropy organization.

One night after our chapter meeting, I went to my mom, frustrated and struggling to put my emotions into words. I was still a teenager, so I wasn't fully versed in how to handle my emotions yet.

In a huff, I vented to my mom that I was frustrated and fed up with this organization. I knew we had put in a lot of years and wanted to see the program through, but I couldn't shake the feeling that I missed what I loved most about it: the volunteer work. I missed helping people.

My mother turned to me and said, "I hear you. I really do. I feel the same way. And while you are dealing with the kids, I'm dealing with the mothers, who are full-grown adults!" This made me chuckle and helped calm me down. "So," she said once she saw I was much calmer, "what do you want to do? We can do volunteer work whenever; just name the date! We don't need a reason to offer our help. But do you want to stay with the organization? It's okay if you don't. I will stand by your decision no matter what."

This was a big shock to me. I knew the whole reason my mom joined in the first place was to bring us closer and give us something to do together since my dad and brother had Boy Scouts. I didn't want to disappoint her, but also we had already put six years into the organization, and I didn't want to leave in the last year. So, I told her I would keep that in mind but would continue to the end.

This is something that I carry with me daily as I learn and collaborate with my clients. I focus on serving my clients and helping their business reach their goals rather than only focusing on my own business goal. More businesses should embrace the mentality of serving others to empower their success. I believe my purpose is to help my clients succeed, a value instilled in me by my mother. I am not in this for my own glorification in design work; I am here to empower others so they feel seen, heard, and valued.

Thank you so much for reading my chapter centered around heartfelt business leadership. I hope you learned some valuable soft skills that you can easily implement into the success and growth of your organization. People want to connect with people, now more than ever. It is up to us to help cultivate our business relations and step into leadership driven by heart.

Katie Smetherman Holmes is the founder and CEO of Brand Studio Creative. She has a master's degree in brand management and communications. She's an award-winning designer and an international best-selling author. Katie mastered the art of transforming brand visions into stunning realities. Her journey in brand marketing and strategy goes beyond the conventional; she has been the architect of complete brand systems for large corporate businesses as well as small boutiques. Her mission is to create real, authentic brands and websites that not only look great but are driven by heart, purpose, and strategy regardless of size or location. Katie will craft a brand that resonates with your audience and positions you for lasting success. From initial concepts to the launch of your refreshed identity, she is with you every step of the way, ensuring a seamless and impactful journey.

Katie offers many DIY branding resources on her company's website as well as different ways to work together. She loves meeting new people and learning what drives them. Let her make your dream a reality!

Website: www.BrandStudioCreative.com

Instagram
https://www.instagram.com/brandstudiocreative/

Facebook
https://www.facebook.com/brandstudiocreative

LinkedIn
https://www.linkedin.com/company/brand-studio-creative/

Portfolio
https://www.behance.net/SmethermanHolmes/projects

Unapologetically Thriving

BY KRISTIN KEE

Who am I? Many of us ask ourselves this question at one time or another, often when we go through a season of change. What I can tell you is that I am just like you. I am someone with a past, a present, and a constant creation of my future.

My journey has been filled with all types of challenges and experiences: child molestation, sexual assault, growing up with alcoholic parents, surviving an abusive stepfather, having a marriage that ended due to my ex-husband's addiction, and raising my children as a single mom. Don't get me wrong; those were some bleak, sometimes living-in-hell moments—with a few of those being Lifetime Movie Network worthy—but what I realized through it all is that they were moments that happened *for me*, not to me.

This chapter is for every woman who feels weighed down by life's burdens, stuck in survival mode, disconnected from her dreams, and may have even lost hope. I know what this all feels like; more importantly, I know it doesn't have to stay this way.

In this chapter, you will learn a little about me and a lot about you. You will find practical steps to shift you from surviving to thriving. You'll learn how to define what thrive mode looks like for you, take inspired action, and begin creating a life by design. My hope for you is simple: I want you to dream again. I want you to believe in yourself, take bold steps in creating a life that excites you, and realize you are not alone and change is possible. You are capable of so much more than surviving; it's time to step into your thrive mode!

Let's begin.

I remember that feeling of having no dreams, no hope, and being stuck in survival mode, doing whatever I needed to get through each day. What I remember most was the exhaustion of it all. My focus was on the moment-to-moment tasks, and I couldn't even imagine what thriving could look like. My goal was not me; it was to survive long enough to ensure I could set my children up to thrive. My mindset was that I had to make the sacrifice so they would never have to endure what I had experienced. Then, some pivotal moments happened in my life that led me from surviving to thriving. Are you ready, Alice? Yes, let's pretend for a moment we are in *Alice in Wonderland* and we are taking a trip down the rabbit hole together, exploring pivotal moments that shaped the life I am creating. Don't worry; I am not going to spill all the tea (that's reserved for the book I may or may not write someday), but I will share the unexpected, humor-filled rabbit hole version. Curious? Let's dive in.

It all started with something simple. I wanted a foot rub, or, to be more exact, a foot zone (foot zoning is an advanced form of reflexology using the points on the entire body addressing physical, emotional, spiritual, and mental well-being). I began searching for someone to provide this service and had this wild experience while doing so.

As I was surfing the internet, looking for a foot zone, I heard a booming voice in my head, **You need to foot zone.** I was like, *Yeah, that's what I am looking for, a foot zone...* Then again, I heard, **You need to foot zone.** At this point, I felt a little weird and questioned what the heck was happening, but again, I heard, *You need to foot zone.* It was a direct command.

CRAZY! Heck yeah, it was crazy. I hated feet—the thought grossed me out, but what did I do? Well, you know it... I began searching for a school to learn. I finally found one and emailed the instructor to learn when the next session would start, as the website said the current class had already begun. The instructor called me; I remember it was a Thursday, and I was at work. She explained what the class entailed and stated that her website was incorrect—the classes would begin that Monday.

I asked for the cost, and when she gave me the amount, I immediately thought, *Nope, it is my boy's wrestling season, and that costs a lot of money and time that I cannot afford.*

She replied, "I feel like you are meant to be in this class, and we will work on payment arrangements... You need to be here."

WHAT!?! I was stunned, excited, and scared, so I signed up for a class that lasted two days once a month. Oh, and did I mention it was seven hours away from me? Also, my kids thought I was going through a mid-life crisis since they knew how much I hated feet back then, and everyone thought I was nuts to drive seven hours to take a class once a month... Yet this is what led me to become a certified foot zone practitioner and start my own practice. I want to take just a moment to thank Vanessa Wynn Young, the instructor who became my friend and started my transformation. That's not the end, though; it even gets wilder down this little rabbit hole... Are you ready to hear more?

During my training, I met the school's owners, Brad and Susan Noall. We clicked instantly, and they quickly became not only my friends but also my mentors, my whos (more on that later in the chapter), and I trusted them completely. Soon, that trust led down an unexpected path.

One night after zoning clients, I was relaxing in my office, scrolling through Facebook, and I saw Brad doing a Facebook Live. He was mixing something in water and stating all these amazing benefits he was receiving. Curious, I texted him, "What is that?" He just laughed, said he would send me a couple of packets, and that I should call him after I tried them out.

Several days later, I received an envelope from Brad, and after a long evening of foot zoning, I opened the envelope with two packets. There was a note, one packet for me, one for a friend, with directions to drink them over a 20-minute time span. I mixed this packet called Keto/OS and drank as instructed. All of a sudden—no lie—my brain lit up like the Fourth of July. The only way I can explain it is that it felt like my brain was wrapped in plastic wrap before the drink, and after the drink, the plastic wrap was pulled off, a cool stream of water poured over it, and everything was turned on. Colors appeared brighter in my zone room. I felt energized, alive, and happy, and, just like that, I was hooked. By the way, there was no way I would share the second packet. Thank you, Brad and Susan Noall, for being my "whos."

Overnight, I went down a rabbit hole, consuming knowledge of what the heck this drink was, and then found out how to become a full-fledged promoter. I started sharing my experience all over social media because, honestly, I wanted everyone to feel the way I did... alive, energized, brain fog gone, and unstoppable.

Then came the moment that changed everything. A question, the biggest question. The one that shook me out of just getting by and pushed me to learn how to really thrive. It took me from helping corporations and other businesses make money to becoming licensed in the financial industry, teaching and helping regular people like me and you how to grow, protect, and diversify their money, and make it tax-free along the way.

The question in a team Zoom meeting was, "What do you hope and dream for?" I froze. I had no answer. Panic set in, and I literally began to sweat. At that moment, I borrowed the hopes and dreams of someone I admired, tweaking it slightly so it wouldn't feel like I was a complete copycat. That was the first small act—borrowing someone else's vision—that became a part of the framework, a stepping stone to thriving. Borrowing someone else's vision gave me hope, which led me to have a dream that pushed me into thrive mode. Key takeaway: Alice, as we continue our journey together, be open to endless opportunities and possibilities, even in places you wouldn't think of... like looking for a foot rub.

Thrive mode activated!

Now to become the person you need to be to thrive. Remember, life isn't a practice round; this is the real deal! Make each day count by creating a life that's designed to bring you joy, excitement, and adventure. Chase your dreams, try new things, and fill your world with what makes you happy. You only get one life, so live it to the fullest and take inspired action.

The first step is the most important, but it's also the one most of us fear. Here's the thing I can guarantee: If you don't take that step, you're destined to stay stuck. Fear is what holds us back, so let's flip the script on it and make fear stand for Face Everything And Rise. Do it scared... It's okay! By taking that first step, you've got a 50/50 chance of success and a 100% chance to learn, adjust, and grow no matter what. So, take the leap, and start the process of thrive mode by asking yourself these five powerful questions. Set aside five minutes right now to answer them, and don't overthink it; just write whatever comes to mind. You are not aiming for perfection; you are aiming for action. You can always come back after this chapter to refine and clarify your answers.

1. If I could wave a magic wand, what does my ideal life look like?

Define what "thriving" means for me: career, relationships, health, finances, happiness.

2. What areas of my life feel unbalanced or unfulfilling?

Identify where I am merely surviving and need growth.

3. What daily habits or mindset shifts can move me toward my goals?

Identify the small, consistent actions that will lead me to big changes.

4. What obstacles or fears are holding me back?

Recognize barriers and then create small action steps to overcome them.

5. Who or what can support me on this journey?

Surround myself with people, resources, and opportunities that uplift me. I don't need to know everything. I need the right "who" or "whos" to help me in my journey to thrive mode.

Now that you have an idea of what thrive mode may look like for you, it's time to continue down our rabbit hole. Remember, we are not chasing perfection; we are creating the framework. And let's be honest, we can't thrive if we are without hope or a dream.

Maybe you can relate to this: the feeling of having no hope and no dream. If you can't relate to this, I am beyond happy for you. But if you can, then you know that it sucks. To have no hopes or dreams is rough. And if you are anything like I was, the way I handled it was by wearing a mask. My mantra (and trust me, I have some past employees who can back me up on this) was, "Fake it 'til you make it." Which is what I did when I borrowed someone else's dream. Good thing or bad thing... hmmm... I am still not sure. I have mixed feelings about it, but what I did realize is not everyone starts with a crystal clear dream, and that is 100% okay. Sometimes, the first step is borrowing someone else's dream and using their vision as a spark to ignite your own.

The truth is, even the most successful people didn't always know exactly where they were headed; they just started somewhere. So, if you're ready to take the leap, here are three inspired action steps I took that can help you, too.

1. Find a mentor or role model.

Look for someone whose dream or journey resonates with you. Use their story to inspire and guide you, but don't compare your life to theirs. What you're seeing is the highlight reel, not the behind-the-scenes struggles. Just like you, they're human with flaws and obstacles to overcome. Your circumstances, skills, and resources may be different, and that's okay. Remember: Comparison is the thief of joy. Let their success ignite your vision.

2. Take bold, imperfect action.

Action creates clarity, plain and simple. Start by diving into activities that inspire you, or better yet, the ones that make you squirm. Why? Because growth doesn't happen when you are comfortable; it happens when you're out there, feeling awkward, unsure, and maybe even scared. Take imperfect action and do it scared! Perfection does not exist!

Now for a reality check; I just want to prepare you. Sometimes—okay, not going to lie—most of the time, the people closest to you won't support your dreams. *OUCH*, I know. But guess what... It's totally okay. You're not here to prove anything to them; you're here to prove it to yourself. They see who you are today, not the incredible person you're becoming. Their doubts? That's about them, not you.

Take it from me; I've been there. I still remember the day I posted my first social media post about a ketone drink. The comments started rolling in: "Ohhhh, so you're trying to be an influencer now?" Then there was the time I opened my foot zoning business and was told, "That'll never work; no one's going to come to you." And when I became a licensed financial professional? Let's just say the skepticism hit new heights. Even now, with a track record of helping people succeed, I still hear remarks from some of the same people. And guess what? It is fine. You know why? Because I am fine and I am in my thrive mode. As a matter of fact, as Mel Robbins says, "Let them. Then let me." **Side note:** I highly recommend reading her book, *The Let Them Theory*. So go ahead; take bold, messy, imperfect action and do it scared. The key is to begin.

3. Refine and personalize your dream.

As you explore, take note of what excites you and what sets your soul on fire. Over time, you'll shape those sparks into a dream that's uniquely yours.

Last but not least, give yourself grace. Your dream does not need to be fully formed today. Just BEGIN in the direction that excites you and know it will change and finally emerge into a vision that is authentically yours.

Alright, let's pause and do a quick recap. So far, you've formed the framework of what thrive mode looks like for you, and you've got three inspired action steps to start fueling those hopes and dreams. Now what?

It's time to starve the distractions, feed the focus, and get serious about figuring out who you are and what you want. Sounds easier said than done, right? Wrong!

Listen carefully, dear Alice (yes, I'm calling you Alice because we're still exploring this rabbit hole together). In fact, grab a highlighter right now because what I'm about to say is highlight-worthy.

If I don't stop and put the oxygen mask on myself first and focus on me instead of everything and everyone else... I will stay stuck in survival mode. Today, and only today, I will demand more for myself because I am worth it.

I AM WORTH IT!

Let that sink in. Highlight it. Write it down and repeat it for the next 30 days. Thriving isn't about doing everything for everyone else; it's about making yourself a priority. You're not just worth it. You deserve it.

Step 1: Quit comparing yourself to others.

Seriously, stop it. As a single mom, I was the queen of comparison. I measured my life against everyone else's highlight reels and convinced myself I was falling short. I compared my family to two-parent households, equating single parenthood with failure. Was I dumb? Yes!

Some of those comparisons came from the stories I told myself, and others came from things people outright said to me:

"You can't be successful without a partner at home to help you."
"Your kids won't do well in school or sports because they're from a broken home."
"Are all your kids from the same dad?"
"She must've made some poor choices to still be single."

How many times have you compared your life to someone else's?

Here's the truth: Once I stopped comparing, I was able to see my life for what it was. I looked at my family, my kids, and myself, and I realized something huge. My circumstances didn't *define* my success; they *refined* it.

Every challenge I faced shaped me into something better. It took my mindset from *"This is impossible"* to *"I'm possible."* And you know what else I realized? We were doing just as well, if not better, than those families I used to compare us to.

Why? Because of our core values as a family. We were a team and committed to each other even during the hardest of times.

Once I embraced what I had right in front of me, I began to fall in love with my life again, and more importantly, I started to fall in love with myself again.

Step 2: Take a social media fast for 30 days.

Social media can be great, but it's a double-edged sword when you keep scrolling and comparing your journey to everyone else's highlight reel. Take some time and give yourself the space to focus on your own growth. If you have to be on social media because that's your job, then get on, post, and get off. No scrolling!

Step 3: Prepare yourself mentally for moments of isolation and know that's totally okay.

There will be times when you question if you're doing the right thing, and that is perfectly normal. It might even get a little harder before it gets easier. I love using the analogy of a rubber band: the more resistance you feel, the further it'll snap you forward once you let go. It's uncomfortable, but that's how growth happens. By pushing through the tension, we get propelled forward to meet a target we once thought was beyond our reach.

Step 4: After your social media fast, surround yourself with like-minded people.

It's incredible what happens when you stop comparing yourself to others and start focusing on your own path. You'll find that people who are on the same journey are naturally attracted to you. If this sounds a little scary or you're unsure of where to start, don't worry, I've got you covered. Listen to my podcast, *Into the Wild: Untamed & Unfiltered*, or join my Facebook Group of the same name and connect with a tribe of bold, fearless women who are ready to collaborate, grow, and support you as you continue to evolve.

Alright, Alice, I can already hear you asking, "Kristin, this all sounds great, but how do I actually feed my focus?" Well, let me tell you, it's simpler than you think. You see, we're not just feeding focus here. We're marrying the activity and divorcing the results. It's not about point A to point Z; it's about what happens in between. The trials, the tribulations, the learning, and the growing are all your gifts to become more.

The truth is that only focusing on results will get you stuck. We are human, and when we only focus on results, we begin wondering if it's all worth it, and we find ourselves frustrated and wanting to give up. Not convinced? Let me prove it to you.

Have you ever heard of "ghost fat?" It's when someone's self-image doesn't match the changes they've gone through physically after losing weight. It's a psychological lag that sometimes takes six months or longer for your brain to catch up to the new you, even though everyone else is already seeing the transformation. I know this happened to me when I went through a weight loss journey, and I am sure it has happened to many of you, too.

The sad truth is, results don't always show up on schedule, but consistency is the secret sauce to creating good habits.

Now for the fun part. Starting each day with YOU!

Have you ever heard of *The Miracle Morning* by Hal Elrod? If you haven't, it's another noteworthy book to read—check it out. The book is based on the idea that setting aside time each day to improve yourself can lead to a more successful and fulfilling life. This is how I began feeding my focus by starting every day with me, borrowing ideas from *The Miracle Morning*, and then creating my DMOs (Daily Modes of Operation).

Every morning before you begin your day, you're going to read this little mantra for the next 30 days:

"Today my focus is creating good habits, not stressing over bad ones. I release the bad habits and will not stress over results. They do not serve me; they only distract me from my thrive mode journey."

After you read this mantra, pick one of the DMOs from the list below and start with just 10 minutes a day. Do that every day for 30 days. As you get comfy, gradually add more from the DMO list until you're spending a solid 30–60 minutes a day in your Thrive Mode. Think of it as a morning ritual broken into little intervals.

Here's your DMO list to choose from:

- **Prioritize your day.** Time blocking is how I set up my day, and it has been a game changer.
- **Read 10 pages of a self-development book daily.**
- **Meditate/visualize/sit in silence for a bit every day.**

- **Journal, express gratitude, or write daily affirmations.**
- **Move your body and hydrate.**
- **And two non-negotiables:** Ask yourself these two questions every morning. I recommend keeping a journal so you can bear witness to your transformation:
  - *"How can I show up today in a way that aligns with my purpose and values?"* This shifts your focus from chasing results to living with intention.
  - *"What is one lesson I can embrace today that will help me grow?"*

This reframes your mindset from measuring success to learning and evolving.

As you start your DMOs, there's something really important I want you to be aware of. By completing them, you create self-awareness, self-compassion, and self-care. Together, these three things create a powerful formula for positive psychology that can help you stay in thriving mode every day. This is not about checking off tasks; it's about building a strong and positive mindset that will keep you thriving each and every day.

I want you to know that you are not meant to fit into society's mold. You are meant to break it. This whole chapter is about you embracing your true self, creating your life by design, and stepping boldly into the life you were made for. This chapter is a call to action for you to live in your power, in your thrive mode, unapologetically and authentically.

We have made it out of the rabbit hole together, and I hope this chapter has lit a fire in you to move from surviving to thriving. Thank you for showing up for yourself and diving into this chapter together. That alone proves you are ready to create and live in thrive mode.

Let's keep this conversation going! Join my Facebook group, where women are supporting each other, collaborating, and growing together. Tune in to my podcast, *Into the Wild: Untamed and Unfil-*

tered, for more bold insights and raw conversations. If you're ready to take control of your financial future, I'd love to offer you a complimentary financial consultation to help you get there. Of course, let's connect on social media—follow me for more inspiration, insights, and real talk.

Kristin Kee is a licensed Financial Professional with a B.A. in Business Administration and a certified Foot Zone Practitioner who specializes in guiding women from financial overwhelm to financial empowerment. As a published author, she is dedicated to helping women break free from societal pressures and unrealistic expectations, creating a lifestyle by design where financial security and freedom go hand in hand.

Kristin's approach is anything but conventional. She doesn't just talk about money; she teaches how it actually grows, how to best protect it, and how to ease the burden of taxes, all through practical, easy-to-implement strategies that aren't taught in traditional finance. Kristin takes the "hard" out of financial planning and replaces it with clarity, confidence, and action.

A mother of four adult children, one bonus child, and a soon-to-be grandmother, Kristin understands the power of resilience and reinvention. She is passionate about equipping women with the knowledge and tools to protect, grow, and create a tax-free wealth plan, transforming their financial future from surviving to thriving. She has an unwavering passion for making a difference and believes that financial freedom is a right, not a privilege, and is why she provides complimentary financial planning.

If you're ready to take control of your finances and build a life on your terms, visit my website to explore a complimentary financial consultation or how we can work together.

Let's make it happen!

For more information or to reach Kristin, visit:
Kristin's website: https://krisbkee.com/home

Follow on

Facebook: Personal
https://www.facebook.com/kristin.brockkee/
or join her facebook community at
https://www.facebook.com/share/g/1B3R2Kje7L/

Instagram
https://www.instagram.com/kristinbrockkee/

TikTok
https://www.tiktok.com/@krisbkee?_t=ZP-8toRrrEJsit&_r=1

The Chakra Codes: Unlock Your Rich Girl Energy

BY MARISSA AULOURE

Our energy holds the keys to unlocking everything we need—like a secret language created within our soul, a sacred code that will open the door to all of your deepest desires, dreams you envision, and the life you are meant to live. This sacred code is embedded in your being, which guides you through all of your decision-making, challenges, and opportunities. This is the energy that has been programmed within you; it's your alignment and your passion, and it leads you to unlock your purpose. It's your chakras! These spinning energy discs inside your body hold the key to unlocking your fullest potential.

You're invited to *The Chakra Codes*, where your energy guides you to create the business and life of your dreams, not just by strategy but from your soul. **Life = Business**, and both are a beautiful reflection of one another and woven into the fabric of your being. When you are in full alignment, you feel lighter and happier; things feel effortless because the energy is attracting and guiding your success. When energy blocks show up, they lower the vibration of our bodies, our mindsets, and our emotions, slowing down the manifestation and abundance we are destined for in our businesses.

I'm Marissa Auloure, a New York native turned Florida beach

lover, a mother of twins, and a psychic business mentor who has helped women create the business and life of their dreams by balancing their chakras and unlocking the gifts that already exist within them. My journey is like an *unalome*, a Buddhist symbol that represents the journey of life with ups and downs, fears, struggles, and directions I did not think my life would take. I knew something within me was special, but my intuitive gifts were not something I was easily able to recognize from the start. Life had a way of awakening what lies within the depths of my soul, a beam of light that needs to shine bright. It began first through motherhood, then through my branding and website creation designs, and last but not least, through the realization that our energy is a direct correlation to the business strategy, which will propel us forward.

If you take anything away from this chapter, I hope it's the understanding that everything you need in life and business is already within you. This is why I wrote this chapter, to share my "aha" moment that all we have to do is look inside ourselves and we will find the answer. When we seek outside validation, it is only our ego needing to be fed. Success is something you unlock; it's not something you chase. Your seven chakras hold the keys to understanding how to identify, release, and balance what's holding you back from your greatest success in life and business. The true secret is mastering your energetic alignment, which is a roadmap to your soul and how you step into flow, ease, and luxury—yes, luxury! Because, why not? Your life and your business can be beautiful, sexy, and chic, and you should feel fabulous in all aspects of yourself.

This chapter is for the woman who is ready to embrace all her desires and *knows* she is ready for more. She feels it in her being, deep in her soul, a yearning for the life that has already been programmed into every cell. She is ready to trust the wisdom within her and stop looking outwards for external validation, guidance, and decision-making. *The Chakra Codes* guides you to uncover energetic patterns that have been influencing your business, identify the blocks that keep you playing small, and clear those blocks that have been keeping you from your greatest success. Chakra energy helps you scale to new heights, unlock your confidence, and ignite your power.

It's your time to truly shine!

Trusting yourself can be a bit scary, but I don't just teach energy work; I live it too. I use it firsthand in my life and business, and my psychic abilities have allowed me to see far beyond just the surface, deep into the soul blueprints of each client's success. When women work with me, they experience the most profound shifts. Shifts they didn't realize they needed or were even possible. It's not just about identifying how you are currently feeling and what needs to be shifted; it's deeper than that—unlocking ancestral karmic blocks, awakening soul-aligned business strategies, and unleashing quantum leaps in money and success. Your energy will always tell the truth, and it's also hard to ignore, especially moments where it feels like it is literally screaming at you. When your body and mind finally align with the frequency your soul already knows, everything expands: your joy, your money, your purpose, your life, and yes, even your business will scale to new heights.

If you are ready to step into the highest version of yourself, claim the life you were meant to live, and ignite the business that will change not only your life but also those of others around you, I'm blessed to be your guide. It's time for us to begin. The answers you've been searching for already have a home within you, and they are ready to be unlocked. Grab your coffee, tea, champagne, or sparkling water (my preferred choice) because it's time for us to step into your luxe life with *The Chakra Codes!*

The First Chakra
The Root Chakra: The Grounding Foundation of Life and Business
Color: Red
Element: Earth
Location: Base of spine
Sanskrit Word: Muladhara

Energy Center: Safety, security, stability, money, self-worth, and ancestral lineage
Crystals to Heal the First Chakra: Ruby, Garnet, Bloodstone, Black Tourmaline, Red Jasper
Essential Oils to Heal the First Chakra: Patchouli, Rosemary, Sandalwood, Myrrh
Foods to Heal the First Chakra: Red Meats, Soy, Tofu, Eggs, Beans, Beets

The Root Chakra and Your Life

Your root chakra is developed before you even take your first breath; from the point of conception, your Root Chakra is already beginning to form. This chakra is your foundation center, which finishes its development around the age of seven. This chakra holds the deep, subconscious programming passed through generations of your family lineage. It's directly associated with your sense of safety, your relationship with money, and your beliefs about feeling secure in the world.

Take a moment and think back to your childhood. What stories did you hear about money, stability, survival, and safety? Did financial stress surround your atmosphere? Did you hear the phrases "Money doesn't grow on trees" or "You have to work hard to earn money"? Even while you were developing in the womb, you received energy from your mother—anything she experienced was programmed into your cells, any experience of fear, financial hardship, or instability. You were born holding generational beliefs about security, abundance, and self-worth all before you were even you and before you had a chance to create your own reality.

The Root Chakra is crucial, as it's the energetic home of your very foundation; without a strong foundation, life and business can feel unstable.

The Root Chakra and Your Business

If your Root Chakra is blocked or unstable, it will show up in your business as feeling "stuck." Your business is a reflection of your energy, which is why I use the phrase "Life = Business."

Questions For The Root Chakra

- Do you struggle with undercharging for your services because deep inside, you don't feel worthy of being able to receive all you desire?
- Do you find yourself experiencing the rollercoaster of money where it flows in, and then suddenly you hit a low where no money is coming to you?
- Do you fear never having enough money, therefore you are afraid to make big investments in your business?
- Do you fear being seen because you feel unsafe, therefore never fully showing up as the leader in your niche?

All of these are signs of an unbalanced and blocked Root Chakra. The term "not enough" is directly associated with this energy center when it is out of alignment, leaving you constantly feeling like you do not have enough money, clients, confidence, or trust in yourself. You may have a hard time pricing your offers or taking bold risks in business and find yourself working from a scarcity mindset.

Healing and Strengthening Your Root Chakra

The main focus of healing your Root Chakra is reprogramming your foundation: letting go of old beliefs, grounding deep into a new mindset, and having a power of money story.

Here's How to Heal the Root Chakra

Rewrite Your Money Story: Identify your limiting beliefs around money and security. Replace those limiting beliefs with grounding affirmations like "I am safe. I am supported. Money easily flows to me. I am a money magnet."

Ground Your Energy Daily: The Root Chakra is your grounding center and directly associated with the earth. Practice walking barefoot on the earth, spending time in nature, or meditating with grounding crystals like black tourmaline or garnet to facilitate healing the root chakra strengthening your foundation.

Clear Generational Patterns: Your money story was externally created by your family and did not start with you. Journal or use guided meditations to connect with your ancestral wounds and start to ground and heal your belief in abundance and security.

Create Safety in Your Business: Set up supportive structures to create a solid financial foundation. Set clear pricing of your services, automate savings, and establish a steady flow of income so you feel secure in your life and your business.

Activate Your Root Chakra With Journal Prompts

1. What money story did I hear growing up?
2. Where do I feel most unstable or have fear in my business?
3. Starting today, how can I create a stronger foundation in my life and business?
4. If I fully trusted I was financially stable and energetically supported, what would my business look like?

A balanced Root Chakra will show up as feeling *safe, confident, and grounded*. You trust you are fully supported, and abundance flows to you. You believe in your worth and build a business that is grounded, stable, and successful.

The Second Chakra
The Sacral Chakra: Unleashing Your Creativity, Passion, and Pleasure
Color: Orange
Element: Water
Location: Between the root chakra and the navel
Sanskrit Word: Swadhisthana
Energy Center: Pleasure, Creativity, Femininity
Crystals to Heal the Second Chakra: Amber, Citrine, Orange Carnelian, Orange or Coral Calcite
Essential Oils to Heal the Second Chakra: Orange, Sandalwood, Clary Sage, Neroli, Yang Ylang
Foods to Heal The Second Chakra: Omega-3 fatty acids, carrots, mango, oranges, apricots, sweet potatoes, peaches, walnuts, flax and chia seeds

The Sacral Chakra and Your Life

Your Sacral Chakra is the center of your creativity, pleasure, and emotional flow. This chakra is deeply connected to your womb space and feminine energy. This chakra holds wound imprints that relate to your mother, sister, or other women in your life.

Take a moment and ask yourself these questions: Have you ever noticed it's easier to get along with men than women? Do you find yourself resisting support from other women or struggling to trust female friendships? If yes, this is often a sign of a mother or sister wound, which are energetic blocks that reside around past experiences with women that you are holding on to.

Many women unconsciously sit in their masculine energy more than their feminine energy because society has conditioned us to believe that femininity is weak. Therefore, we find it easier to sit in our masculine energy, pushing, forcing, and overworking because we are conditioned to believe that is the only way to get ahead in life and succeed.

The truth is that true power lies in the "balance." You unlock a state of flow when you embrace your feminine energy. This is where ease, creativity, and inner knowing (your intuition) guide your journey, instead of sitting in burnout and control. As women in business and life, allowing ourselves to be in our divine feminine energy is where we thrive.

The Sacral Chakra and Your Business

The Sacral Chakra shapes how your business looks, feels, and connects with others—it is the creative heart and soul of your brand.

Questions for the Sacral Chakra

- Do you struggle with defining your brand identity?
- Do you feel blocked with creating content and expressing yourself online?
- Are you afraid to be seen? To share your story, express yourself, and put your essence into your brand?
- Do you feel like your business has become more task-filled rather than passion-driven and disconnected from the joy of your business?

If any of these resonate with you, your Sacral Chakra may be out of balance and out of alignment. When your Sacral Chakra is blocked, it can show up as signs of creative stagnation, self-doubt, and your brand feels disconnected from who you truly are.

Your branding is a direct reflection of your Sacral energy. The way your logo looks, the colors you select and the language you use, along with the overall aesthetic of your business, conveys and evokes an emotion that comes from you and connects with your audience. If you struggle with brand clarity and feel uninspired, this will have an effect on attracting your ideal clients.

Your brand will feel magnetic when your Sacral Chakra is balanced. When you infuse your energy into your business, you make it irresistible for those who want to work with you, resulting in a "heck yes!" answer from them.

Healing and Strengthening Your Sacral Chakra

Connect with Your Feminine Energy: Your feminine energy is fluid, not meant to be forced. Move your body, dance, do yoga, tap into pleasure and sensuality, and allow yourself to move in a flowing way without structure.
Heal Your Mother/Sister Wound: Give thought to any past pain that is related to female relationships, whether this be with your mother, sister, female friends, or even other women you have interacted with, and begin to rewrite your story. Surround yourself with women who lift you up, support you, and empower you to truly shine in your growth.
Ignite Your Creativity: The more you allow yourself to "play," the easier it is to be creative and allow your creative side to flow freely. Draw, paint, write, sing, and create without any judgment or expectations, and express yourself through the activity of art.
Embody and Infuse Your Brand with Your Essence: If you find that your brand feels disconnected and lacks that magnetic "wow" that lights you up, revisit your colors, logo, and visuals. Ask yourself: Does this truly feel like me? Is this how I want my business to feel? Your business should visually and emotionally align with your true energy.

Activate Your Sacral Chakra With Journal Prompts

1. What beliefs do I hold about feminine energy? Do I see feminine energy as weak or powerful?
2. How do I feel about my relationships and connections with other women?
3. In my business, where do I feel creativity blocked or uninspired?

4. If I fully embodied my authentic essence, what would my brand look and feel like?
5. When it comes to pleasure and passion, how can I invite more of it into my work and daily life?

When your Sacral Chakra is balanced, open, and fully thriving, your business brand and life become a beautiful work of art. Your creativity is flowing effortlessly, you receive new ideas easily, and your business forms into a creative, authentic expression of your deep desires and visions. The real focus and realization to feel within this chakra is that you are no longer forcing your success, but you are attracting and magnetizing your success.

The Third Chakra
The Solar Plexus Chakra: Confidence and Personal Power
Color: Yellow
Element: Fire
Location: Between the navel and sternum
Sanskrit Word: Manipura
Energy Center: Confidence, personal power, inner child, self-worth, joy and action
Crystals to Heal the Third Chakra: Citrine, Tiger's Eye, Yellow Tourmaline
Essential Oils to Heal the Third Chakra: Lemon, Chamomile, Bergamot, Cedarwood, Rosemary
Foods to Heal The Third Chakra: Lemons, Corn, Pineapple, Squash, Turmeric, Ginger, Banana, Brown Rice, Sunflower Seeds, Barley

The Solar Plexus Chakra and Your Life

The Solar Plexus Chakra is your power center. This chakra directly connects to your confidence, personal power, and ability to take action, and it is deeply connected to your inner child. Your inner child is the part of you that was once free, playful, and fearless before conditioning and external expectations from society took over.

As children, it is our natural ability to run, play, explore, feel free, and create without hesitation or concern that we are doing it wrong. We dance without caring how we look to others, sing without worrying if our pitch is perfect, and allow ourselves to express how we feel freely. As we grow up, we start to look outwards for validation and seek approval from others before we take action, worrying that it might be wrong or what others will think.

- Do you fear the judgment of what others will think and, therefore, hold yourself back?
- Do you struggle with self-worth? Do you hesitate to take up space?
- Do you seek reassurance before making a decision?

If you answered yes to any of these questions, then your Solar Plexus Chakra may be blocked. Childhood wounds and self-doubt sit directly in this chakra and are formed between childhood and teenage years. Those experiences may still be shaping how you show up in your life today, with a sensitivity to criticism, being overlooked, or being made to feel like you are "too much" or "not enough."

The child within you does not need external validation or approval. Your inner child simply wants to create, play, and express themselves, which brings joy. To heal the Solar Plexus Chakra you must reconnect with your inner child and embrace what she needs.

The Solar Plexus Chakra and Your Business

Your Solar Plexus Chakra transforms all of your ideas (Sacral Chakra) and turns them into action, making this chakra the chakra of execution. If your business is feeling stuck, unstructured, or unclear, this chakra may need some TLC and balancing.

Questions for the Solar Plexus Chakra

- How are you showing up in your business?
    - If you find yourself struggling with marketing, website messaging, or showing up online, these are signs of an imbalance in the Solar Plexus. You fear you are not the expert in your field, doubting yourself and comparing yourself to others instead of fully embracing and having fun with your unique gifts.
- Do you feel disconnected from your offers/services?
    - In business, this chakra represents your services, program, and business model. If you find that you are second-guessing yourself and what to offer, you may be building and creating from a place of looking outwards at what others are doing instead of what truly excites you and is coming from you.
- Does the thought of taking bold action scare you?
    - If you hesitate to launch a new program, increase your prices, or put yourself out there, your confidence needs strengthening. You must shine bright, reclaim the inner fire that already exists within you, and trust your instincts.

Healing and Strengthening Your Solar Plexus Chakra

Connect with Play and Joy: Engage in activities that make you feel light, happy, playful, excited, and joyful. Activities may be dancing, painting, or simply laughing; feeling joy fuels your confidence.
No More Seeking External Validation: Connect inwards and challenge yourself to make decisions based on what feels good and right for you, not seeking approval based on what others think.
Declare Your Power: Speak your power into action by reminding yourself daily. "I am worthy. I am capable. I am confident."

It's Time for Imperfect Action: Your confidence grows by "doing." Take all the risks, stop waiting until everything is perfect; believe in yourself. Do the thing! Launch the program! Post the content! Take the leap!

Stop the Comparison: Look inwards to create, not outwards. Stop looking at what others are doing. Connect to your soul, connect to your body, connect to your essence, and ask yourself: What excites me? What would I create if I had no fear?

Activate Your Solar Plexus Chakra with Journal Prompts

1. As a child, what brought me joy? Thinking about that energy, how can I bring that energy into my business?
2. Due to fear and judgment, where am I holding back in my life and business?
3. Where in my business do I feel the least confident and why?
4. What would I create if I fully trusted myself?
5. Without overthinking, where can I take one bold step today?

When your Solar Plexus Chakra is strong and secure, you embody inner strength and show up in your life and business with boldness and certainty. You create from within and do not wait for permission; you just show up and do it. You lead and don't compare. When you do this, your energy is vibrant, joyful, and magnetic, drawing in effortless success towards you.

The Fourth Chakra
The Heart Chakra: Unlock Love, Compassion, and Abundance
Color: Green (or Pink)
Element: Air
Location: Heart (center of your chest)
Sanskrit Word: Anahata
Energy Center: Love, compassion, self-acceptance, boundaries, relationships, healing
Crystals to Heal the Fourth Chakra: Rose quartz, jade, green calcite, green tourmaline, green aventurine, emerald, malachite
Essential Oils to Heal the Fourth Chakra: Lime, rose, jasmine, eucalyptus, lavender, helichrysum
Foods to Heal The Fourth Chakra: Kale, spinach, broccoli, celery, cucumber, zucchini, matcha, lime, mint, peas, green apples, avocado, green tea

The Heart Chakra and Your Life

The Heart Chakra is the connection between your physical and spiritual self and holds the energy of love, self-love, compassion, forgiveness, and connection. The ability to love and receive love unconditionally is rooted deep within this chakra, but this is also where wounds are located for many.

We often struggle with giving ourselves love, but we find it easier to love others freely. Why is that? This chakra prompts you to ask yourself:

- How do you speak to yourself? Are you harsh on yourself?
- Do you hold on to pain and resentment?
- Do you struggle with boundaries and self-love?

Many of us can easily relate to the wounds of the heart chakra from past experiences such as heartbreak, betrayal, loss, or rejection. We hold onto this pain because it is familiar when we should really be releasing it. When we forgive, we free ourselves from the weight of it, which does not mean we are excusing what happened, but healing for ourselves and no one else.

This chakra has a strong connection to animals and nature. Animals embody unconditional love and love without expectations. Let nature nurture your heart chakra back to love by spending time with animals, walking barefoot on the earth, or even sitting under the trees. Allow Mother Nature to heal your heart wounds.

The Heart Chakra and Your Business

How you give, receive, and interact in your business is all determined by the energy of your Heart Chakra. If this chakra is blocked and out of balance, you may experience:

- **Feeling like you are pouring from an empty cup and that you are "giving the house away"**
    - You tend to overgive, undercharge for your worth, and feel drained. You struggle with saying no, along with pricing and creating boundaries.
- **Resistant to offering value for free**
    - You are afraid to give away freebies, lead magnets, or helpful content because you are fearful that if you give too much, you will not have anything to receive in return.
- **Lack of Trust**
    - If you have been burned before, your Heart Chakra holds on to the pain. This may be clients not paying you, people taking advantage, and partnerships falling apart. This creates resistance to connection, collaboration, and feeling generous to give.
- **Difficulty Setting Boundaries**
    - You want to help everyone and become a people pleaser, but by doing so you are neglecting yourself.

This can lead to resentment, exhaustion, frustration, and anger.

Oftentimes, if the Heart Chakra is imbalanced, it ties back to the Root Chakra. Do you feel safe to receive? Do you believe you are worthy to receive?

Finding a balance between giving and receiving in business will heal the Heart Chakra. You do not need to self-sacrifice to serve others, and you can be generous to others without depleting yourself.

Healing and Strengthening Your Heart Chakra

Practice Forgiveness and Self-Love: Speak more kindly to yourself and release past wounds. Choose to let go and move forward, and show yourself love.
Connect with Nature and Animals: Animals' energy will heal you because they give us pure love without conditions.
Create From A Place of Love, Not Fear: Remove fear and trust that you can offer value in your business without being taken advantage of. That generosity attracts more abundance.
Remove Guilt and Set Boundaries: You can still honor your limits and give. Saying no is not rejection; it's about having self-respect and honoring what you need.

Affirmations for the Heart Chakra

- *"I feel comfortable giving and receiving love freely."*
- *"I honor myself and set healthy boundaries."*
- *"I am worthy and receive abundance freely."*
- *"Love flows to me and through me effortlessly."*

Activate Your Heart Chakra With Journal Prompts

1. Am I overgiving without receiving in my life and business? If so, where in my life and business am I doing this?
2. What walls do I have up around my heart, and what past experiences have caused this?
3. When it comes to setting boundaries, how can I do this and still feel loving and aligned?
4. When I think about unconditional self-love, what does this mean and look like for me?
5. How can I have an open heart in my business without fear?

When your Heart Chakra is balanced and open, you will find that your life and business flow with more ease. You are able to finally give without fear and receive guilt-free. Your business makes a true impact because you are able to create a space of abundance and genuine connection.

The Fifth Chakra
The Throat Chakra: Activating Your True Voice and Authentic Self-Expression
Color: Blue Turquoise or Aquamarine Blue
Element: Ether (Space)
Location: Throat
Sanskrit Word: Visuddha
Energy Center: Communication, self-expression, truth, confidence
Crystals to Heal the Fifth Chakra: Aquamarine, Lapis Lazuli, blue kyanite, turquoise, sodalite
Essential Oils to Heal the Fifth Chakra: Juniper, Peppermint, Cypress, spearmint, chamomile
Foods to Heal The Fifth Chakra: Blueberries, apples, pears, plums, coconut water, herbal teas, raw honey, lemon

The Throat Chakra and Your Life

The Throat Chakra is your center for your voice, communication, and genuine self-expression. It rules how you speak to yourself and others and how you express "your truth." If this chakra is blocked or out of alignment, it will show up as signs of struggling to speak up, having a fear of judgment, suppressing how you truly feel, and/or avoiding sharing your truth to avoid conflict.

This chakra has a deep connection to the Solar Plexus Chakra, which is your confidence and self-worth center. If you have a hard time believing in yourself (Solar Plexus Chakra), you won't honor your voice and speak your truth (Throat Chakra).

Underactive Throat Chakra Sign

- Difficulty speaking up for yourself
- The fear of being judged or being rejected makes you silence your voice
- You avoid difficult conversations and confrontation
- You feel unheard or undervalued in your relationship

Overactive Throat Chakra Signs

- You do not allow space for others and tend to dominate conversations
- You tend to talk excessively but have a difficult time truly connecting with people
- Rather than taking action, you feel the need to prove yourself through your words

Maybe at some point you were taught that your voice does not matter, or you were told to be quiet, or that your opinions were not of value. When you hold on to this energy, it gets stuck in your throat, making it a struggle to express yourself freely and with confidence.

The Throat Chakra and Your Business

In business, your Throat Chakra impacts how you communicate your brand, your message, and your mission, which is a pretty powerful role. If this chakra is blocked or out of alignment, it will show up in your business as feeling stagnant, unclear, or disconnected from your true authentic voice.

Your Business Messaging and Marketing

- Do you have difficulty finding the right words to describe your business?
- Do you struggle with your content feeling inauthentic or forced?
- Are you afraid to show up and be seen or heard?

Speaking and Visibility in Your Business

- Does the thought of showing up on video, social media, or podcasts give you anxiety or cause hesitation?
- Are you afraid of being judged, so you avoid putting yourself out there?
- Are you afraid to share your personal story and not hold back?

Writing and Content Creation in Your Business

- Do your website, emails, or captions feel unaligned and disconnected from your authentic voice?
- Do you second-guess what you are writing and delay posting?
- Do you have a fear of saying the "wrong" thing?

The throat chakra is about your voice, which is your power. If this chakra is blocked in business, it will show up as a struggle with your marketing, visibility, and/or messaging. When this chakra is balanced and aligned, you will express yourself with confidence, share your authentic voice and story, and connect to your audience authentically and genuinely.

Healing and Strengthening Your Throat Chakra

Remove Fear and Speak Your Truth: Activate your voice and give yourself permission to speak and use your voice. Even when it feels uncomfortable, push yourself to speak up in conversations.
Stop Overthinking and Just Write: Let the words flow freely from you and remove self-judgment: journal, blog, or post on social media—just do the thing!
Implement Conscious Listening: The Throat Chakra isn't just about speaking and being heard it's also about being able to listen. Both sides should be heard and engage in deep conversation; before speaking, listen, process, and then participate.
Sound and Healing Affirmations: Activate the Throat Chakra by using sound to heal. Sing, chant, hum, or repeat affirmations such as, "My voice is beautiful and powerful. There is value in what I have to say. I speak and express my authentic voice with confidence and clarity."
Speak and Create From Your Essence: Show up as authentically YOU! Stop worrying that you have to say it perfectly. The right people who are meant to hear your message will resonate with it.

Activate Your Throat With Journal Prompts

1. Where am I holding back my true voice in my business?
2. How do I want to express myself in my life and in my business?
3. When I think about using my voice, what fears come up?
4. What is the message I feel called to share with the world?

Speaking and writing come easily when your Throat Chakra is open and balanced. Your words are deeply connected to your message, and you find that words flow authentically from you. You own your voice and your power, and you no longer have a fear of being seen or heard.

The Sixth Chakra
The Third Eye Chakra: Clarity of Vision
Color: Indigo
Element: Light
Location: Space between the eyebrows
Sanskrit Word: Anja
Energy Center: Intuition, wisdom, clarity, spiritual vision
Crystals to Heal the Sixth Chakra: Amethyst, charoite, labradorite, lapis lazuli, unakite, turquoise
Essential Oils to Heal the Sixth Chakra: Juniper, frankincense, sandalwood, clary sage (*if you have an overactive third eye chakra, use patchouli)
Foods to Heal The Sixth Chakra: Blueberries, blackberries, purple grapes, plums, purple carrots, elderberries, eggplant, purple potatoes, raisins, figs

The Third Eye Chakra and Your Life

The Third Eye Chakra is the energy center of your inner wisdom, clarity, and intuition. This is where you do not need external validation and trust in yourself because you are able to access your deepest "knowing." This chakra is your "inner sight," guiding you towards your soul's purpose because it helps you recognize where you lack clarity.

If your Third Eye Chakra is blocked, it may show up as

- Feeling indecisive, unsure, scattered, or stuck
- Always seeking external validation and not trusting in your intuition
- Feeling disconnected from your spiritual gifts and your inner wisdom
- Ignoring your gut feeling or spiritual downloads, and over-relying on logic
- Fear of fully stepping into your higher purpose

A balanced Third Eye Chakra will show up as having deep clarity, confidence, and acting in full alignment with your gifts and purpose. In addition, you will trust your instincts, feel the deep connection to your gifts, and be able to make clear decisions easily.

This center is a direct connection to the universe and yourself, which activates your divine wisdom. Your vision becomes more clear when you are aligned with yourself.

The Third Eye Chakra and Your Business

The Third Eye Chakra in business allows you to fully step into your role as a leader through your brand vision and intuitive strategy. When this is open, you connect with your ideal client, confidently sell, and show up as the leader you are meant to be.

Attracting Your Clients and Sales

- When your Third Eye Chakra is balanced, you will easily attract your ideal clients because you have a clear vision and are magnetic about it.
- You feel empowered and are captivating on sales calls; you speak with confidence and certainty.
- You guide your audience naturally because your funnels, emails, and website are set up to flow intuitively.

Step Into Your Leadership

- You show up as the thought leader in your niche or field, because you are owning your expertise and influencing others
- You look inwards and create unique gifts and offers from the downloads you receive and do not copy others.
- You resonate with your audience because your message deeply aligns with your soul.

Your Marketing and Business Growth

- If your marketing feels unclear, scattered, or even uninspired, your Third Eye Chakra may be blocked.
- You may have a difficult time figuring out the right offers, your pricing, and the next steps for you to take.
- When your Third Eye Chakra is balanced and opened, you are able to see the big picture and create your offers from a place that feels inspired, aligned, and powerful.

A Foggy Third Eye = Low Vibration

If you feel lost, uncertain, and disconnected from your business vision, you may be in a low vibrational state, causing your Third Eye Chakra to feel blocked. If you are feeling this way, it may lead to unclear messaging, lack of confidence in your decision-making, and being hesitant with sales.

In order to align your Third Eye Chakra, you must focus on raising your vibration. You begin to do this by trusting your gifts and stepping into your purpose.

Healing and Strengthening Your Third Eye Chakra

It's Time To Trust Your Intuition: Your first instinct is usually right, so stop second-guessing yourself.

Take Time To Meditate and Visualize: Connect with your inner wisdom by sitting in silence.
Pen To Paper and Journal Your Downloads: Put pen to paper and write down your dreams, visions, and intuitive insights.
Bring Awareness to Your Ideal Clients' Energy: What do your clients need from you? How can you help guide them?
Share Your Voice and Sell With Conviction: Stand in your power and own your gifts, and share them with others without hesitation.
Raise Your Divine Vibration: Use activities such as breathwork, sound healing, nature walks, and energy healing to increase your vibration through high-frequency activities.

Affirmations for the Third Eye Chakra

- *"I trust my inner wisdom and my intuition."*
- *"I see my path with clear vision and confidence."*
- *"I am deeply connected to my divine purpose."*

Activate Your Third Eye Chakra With Journal Prompts

1. Where do I feel unclear or uncertain in my business?
2. When making decisions, how can I trust my intuition more?
3. What does my ideal client truly need to hear and see from me?
4. How can I show up with more confidence and sell with conviction and step into leadership?
5. What are the limiting beliefs that are holding me back and blocking me from stepping into my power?

The Seventh Chakra
The Crown Chakra: Divine Purpose and Alignment
Color: Violet or White
Element: Time and space (thought and pure consciousness)
Location: Top of head

Sanskrit Word: Sahasrara
Energy Center: Divine connection, purpose, flow, spiritual alignment
Crystals to Heal the Seventh Chakra: Clear quartz, amethyst, charoite, labradorite, lapis lazuli, unakite, turquoise
Essential Oils to Heal the Seventh Chakra: Juniper, frankincense, basil, rosemary, thyme, clary sage, mugwort, sandalwood (*patchouli if you have an overactive crown chakra)
Foods to Heal The Seventh Chakra: Blueberries, blackberries, purple grapes, plums, purple carrots, elderberries, eggplant, purple potatoes, raisins, figs

The Crown Chakra and Your Life

The Crown Chakra is your connection to universal energy, your highest self, and your divine wisdom. Your soul has a mission, and when your Crown Chakra is balanced, you will feel a sense of peace and trust that life is going exactly as it should be for you.

Blocked Crown Chakra Signs

- You feel disconnected from yourself, from source, your purpose, and the world around you.
- You encounter brain fog, confusion, and lack of direction.
- You do not trust your path and struggle with feeling lost or uninspired.
- You have an increased sensitivity to light and sound
- You feel disconnected from your intuition and are spiritually blocked
- You combat self-doubt and depression, and you question everything around you.

When you lose touch with your spiritual alignment or when you are ignoring your soul's deeper calling and purpose, this chakra tends to get out of balance. Reconnecting with yourself through trust, flow, and divine guidance will help to heal the Crown Chakra.

The Crown Chakra and Your Business

The Crown Chakra is the key that opens the door to aligning with your purpose and truly living it through your business. This chakra governs your inspiration, how well you align with your flow, and your ability to trust in divine timing.

Business Alignment and Flow

- You do not force results when this chakra is open; instead, you trust the road ahead, trust the process, and take inspired action that you know is the right path for you.
- When you are in alignment with your purpose, you know that things will flow to you easily and without resistance.
- There is a bigger mission behind the work that you do. When you are connected to your Crown Chakra, you feel motivated, creative, and connected to the big picture and mission.

Your Clarity, Your Strategy and Planning:

- When your Crown Chakra is blocked, you tend to feel disorganized, lack focus, and struggle with your business direction.
- Your success does not just come from inspiration but also from intentional daily actions. Are you scheduling time to grow your business?

- How are you planning your day, your marketing, and your offers? Are they planned with clarity and purpose?

Facilitate From A Higher Purpose:

- The Crown Chakra is deeply rooted in your purpose and impact and tied to serving others.
- You feel lit up and fulfilled when your business is deeply aligned with your soul purpose mission.
- Your digital presence (website, funnels) and messaging should showcase the higher vision of your mission and inspire others.

Your Community and Your Growth

- How connected are you to your community and ideal clients?
- Are you making an effort to grow your business connections and network daily?
- Are you holding yourself accountable to expand your business and serve your ideal clients?
- Are you upselling clients when the opportunity arises?

The Crown Chakra helps you live with purpose and be in tune with the universe. Your business will feel fully aligned, expansive, abundant, and in flow when the Crown Chakra is balanced. You trust that the universe supports you, has your back when making empowered decisions, and helps you lead from a place of taking inspired action daily.

Healing and Strengthening Your Crown Chakra

Connect With Source Daily: Take the time to recharge and fill up your cup to stay aligned through meditation, prayer, or engage in spiritual practices.

Relinquish Control and Trust: Surrender and release the need for control, and allow the natural flow of abundance to come to you.
Rituals for Clarity: The start of your day should be grounded. To do so, begin your day with setting intentions, journaling, and visualizing.
Create Inspired Action: Stay consistent in your business by planning your business activities, connecting with ideal clients, and networking daily.
Embody Your Purpose: Your soul's mission should align with your business, marketing, and messaging.
Elevate Your Vibration: Participate in high-frequency activities, which include daily gratitude, moving the body, and align with your breath (by practicing breathwork).

Affirmations for the Crown Chakra

- *"I trust the universe has a divine plan in place that is unfolding in my life."*
- *"I am deeply rooted and connected to my purpose and soul mission, and abundance flows easily to me."*
- *"I take daily inspired action to expand my business and serve my community."*

Activate Your Crown Chakra With Journal Prompts

1. In my business, where do I feel disconnected and out of alignment?
2. Am I taking inspired action daily to grow my business? How can I increase this?
3. Am I ignoring big opportunities in my business? What are they?
4. How do I service my ideal clients, and how is this making an impact?
5. How can I start to bring more clarity and flow into my business?

When the Crown Chakra is open, you feel connected to yourself and the world around you, and you operate from a place of trust, flow, and higher purpose to share your mission and vision. The growth and expansion of your business happens fluidly because you are deeply connected to your purpose, you are aligned with service and abundance, and you trust in divine timing.

Ignite Your Power and Align Your Business With Your Divine Energy

Your chakras are more than just energetic spinning discs within your body; they are the blueprint of how you show up in your life and in business. When balanced, you will have clarity and feel aligned and abundant. Not only will you trust yourself, but you will have confidence; you will effortlessly attract positive opportunities and take inspired action that propels you forward. My hope for you is that after reading this chapter, you understand that you hold the very power within you to ignite your dreams, align with your deepest desires, and make the deep connection between your energy and your business, empowering you to take the first step into clearing energetic blocks that are holding you back and fully stepping into your divine purpose.

I'm honored you took this journey with me and excited for what's possible now that you have the tools to unlock your full potential and step into your power with confidence. Remember, you are capable of unleashing and building a business that not only thrives, but is aligned, fulfilling, beautiful, luxurious, and expansive. Continue to integrate the lessons learned in this chapter and all will be possible for you.

My desire is to support you fully; therefore, I have a special gift for you—The Chakra Codes Workbook—a guide to dive even deeper into working with your chakras and begin to directly apply it to your business. Grab your free gift here: https://auloure.com/the-chakra-codes-workbook

If you're feeling lit up and ready to take this transformation to the next level, I invite you to connect with me. We'll indulge in awakening your light, aligning your energy, scaling your business, and stepping confidently into the highest version of yourself. Your highest self is already waiting for you to meet her; let's unlock the door to your power together!

Marissa Auloure is not just a Psychic Business Mentor; she is the visionary force behind the esteemed Auloure Empire. With a wealth of experience as a published author, captivating speaker, acclaimed artist, and astrologer, Marissa brings a multifaceted approach to guiding women toward their highest potential.

Her expertise extends far beyond conventional boundaries. As a seasoned chakra expert, Marissa possesses a profound understanding of energy dynamics, allowing her to facilitate the release of energy blocks and empower women to ascend to the pinnacle of success.

Marissa is also the founder of Auloure, an intuitive drag-and-drop website and business platform designed specifically for women. Auloure empowers entrepreneurs to create professional, energetically aligned websites with ease, providing the tools they need to grow their businesses in alignment with their unique vision and purpose.

Through her transformative guidance, Marissa helps women not only build 7-figure businesses but also do so in complete alignment with their deepest values and aspirations. Drawing upon her intuitive gifts, Marissa channels messages from the divine, igniting the flames of possibility and guiding women toward the realization of their wildest dreams.

Join Marissa on a journey of self-discovery, empowerment, and unparalleled growth as you unlock the secrets to living a life of abundance and fulfillment.

LIMITLESS LEADERSHIP

Website: www.auloure.com
DIY Website Builder: www.auloure.com/builder

Follow On

Facebook
https://www.facebook.com/auloure

Instagram
www.instagram.com/houseofauloure

TikTok
@houseofauloure

Email
hello@auloure.com

Leading From Within

BY MARISSA YUBAS

As a female entrepreneur, I have had a multitude of experiences in modern society—as a business owner, an employee, a stepparent, a spouse, a daughter, and a sister. I have learned a tremendous amount about what society expects of women, how women have been conditioned to think of themselves, and what they've been taught to believe about themselves.

With over 12 years of experience as a licensed therapist and a mindset coach, I have helped countless women redefine success, create growth-oriented mindset shifts, and lean into the authentic persons they really are and who they want to be. Having worked in a variety of settings, I've been able to combine my life experiences with my own therapeutic journey, and I have firsthand experience with the things that I talk about in this chapter.

My purpose for writing this chapter is to empower women to recognize that they have the power to create their best selves and build the best quality of life from the inside out. Women don't need to live their lives for anyone else other than themselves. My ultimate goal of coaching is for women to really connect with the fact that, with a shift in mindset, anything is possible. This chapter is for all women who deal with internal struggles and dissonance and don't feel very good about themselves or are not fulfilled with their lives or careers. I *know* how incredible we are as women and how capable we are of making decisions that support our true selves, allowing us to lead our most successful lives, even beyond our expectations.

I'm right there alongside you. I'm not here to preach. I'm here to help, support, guide, and provide new ideas and perspectives for women who struggle with self-confidence, self-esteem, and hurtful core beliefs.

Readers of this chapter are going to learn how mindset impacts our overall well-being and affects our ability to be successful on our own terms when it comes to our careers and lives. My hope is that women who read my chapter will feel inspired to take action to change their own lives from the inside out for themselves for the sake of their own self-fulfillment. By taking courageous action, women can step into their fullest selves, live a fulfilling life, and reach and exceed their personal goals that feel good to them and put them on track for all that's possible in their lives.

Mindset and perspective shape our realities. The impact of self-perception can have either a helpful or harmful impact on not only our mental well-being and our relationships. Our mindset and perspectives have effects on our careers and our ability to grow throughout life. So, how do we go about recognizing our mindset and those self-limiting beliefs? How do we build a mindset that aligns with what we want to create and our desired realities? We must learn how our mindset can shape our conflict resolution skills and how it impacts the quality and outcome of all of our interactions with different personalities and within ourselves.

The best leaders know both their assets and their liabilities. The reason why that's so important is because when we know who we really are, we can make the best decisions for ourselves, for our loved ones, and for our careers. Women who are effective leaders lean into their nurturing abilities, accept responsibility, and create safe places for others to be their authentic selves. By doing so, women leaders can tap into their unique strengths to bring out the best in the people around them, leading them to more growth and productivity.

It took me a long time to recognize how I had been conditioned to think about myself.

It took me a really long time and a lot of work to learn that those things that I thought about myself were not true and held me back. I had to let go of beliefs and values that weren't true to me. And by doing this, I removed most of my internal dissonance.

I learned that the way I was conditioned to think and feel about myself and the reality of the type of person I was at my core created a lot of tension within me. I really struggled to make decisions and create actions in my life that aligned with who I was, how I wanted to feel about myself, how I wanted to go through life, and how I wanted to interact with other people. Once I learned to be true to myself and my values, the number of opportunities that opened for me personally and professionally was immense.

I had to overcome common issues like an inferiority complex, imposter syndrome, scarcity mindset, and self-limiting beliefs. Having an inferiority complex means that we believe that we are less than others. Experiencing imposter syndrome means we don't believe that we are good enough at what we do and feel like we're just pretending to know what we're doing. A scarcity mindset is a way of thinking that focuses on what we lack rather than what we have. And my core beliefs came from what I learned from other people, society as a whole, and marketing. While watching and listening to others, including the media, I was taught that if I didn't look a certain way, act a certain way, drive a certain car, or if my family didn't behave a certain way, that meant something was wrong with me.

It's easy to get caught up with chasing what we *think* we should be rather than focusing on who we are as unique women. I learned that those things I was conditioned to believe and seek to achieve didn't necessarily align with my values. That's an example of being conditioned on how to think and perceive myself in the world, and as a result, my value as a person was skewed. By overcoming those beliefs, I learned not only is it possible to change my beliefs about myself, but it's a compelling process.

In terms of a scarcity mindset, I learned that if I didn't have enough of this or that material thing, then my life wasn't complete. That's simply not true. I realized that having a fulfilling life comes from my mindset, my perspective, my beliefs, and my values. Fulfillment comes from a place of inner security and peace. It's easy to be fooled into believing that to have a full life, we need to fill it with "things." How has that been working out for us so far? Shifting away from a scarcity mindset moves us toward an abundance mindset. Through an abundance mindset, we start to believe that there's enough to go around! We move through life with a mind open to new possibilities that may arise at any given time. We move from worrying about lost opportunities and believing nothing like that will come around again to thinking that this "lost" opportunity is just a stepping stone, helping us move forward in life and looking forward to what may be coming down the line instead of ruminating on the past and the "what ifs."

I learned how to build my self-esteem and self-confidence through this awareness. As I released the burden of other people's beliefs, fears, and biases, I became more aware and accepting of my strengths and weaknesses. By recognizing them, I'm now able to leverage my personal assets for growth in all areas of my life. And by acknowledging and accepting my weaknesses, I've learned that those weaknesses don't have to be my downfall. They are jumping points where I can use my strengths, assets, values, and mindset to focus on where I want more growth and change so that I can turn those weaknesses into assets. I can shift my mindset and perspective and recognize that having weaknesses simply means I am human. Human beings are fallible. The areas where I have more room to grow are merely areas where I can apply my skills toward learning and personal growth and development. My perceived weaknesses and failures no longer need to be a cage that keeps me imprisoned. I hold the key, and that key is a growth mindset.

We are not perfect. It's not possible to be perfect. I'm able to recognize how my mindset can hold me back. And this is a big part of my coaching. We go through and discover what our values are. We learn how to create action to *show up* and *live* on purpose through what we value most. We let go of the values that we were living by that didn't align with who we are and who we want to be. We figure out how we can apply action steps toward our values so we can make different decisions to change how we move through our lives. When we live according to our values, we build our self-esteem, confidence, inner peace, serenity, contentment, and overall fulfillment because we start to truly and completely live our lives for ourselves, not for others.

We increase our self-confidence because we are living for ourselves. We are accomplishing things and creating and nurturing a life from the inside out that will open the door to new possibilities. I see so many women in my work who are afraid to step into their feminine energy and leadership.

When people, including ourselves, are seen and heard, we let down our defenses. We're more open-minded to hearing feedback. When we can be in that position where we are out of our defenses and into our intuition, we grow as people in all areas of our lives. We help encourage others to step up in their own lives. And we realize intuition is so powerful. It's what makes us unique. We can learn to use our intuition along with a mindset shift to be super effective in making big strides in life and interpersonal relationships. We can find balance in our lives and become very effective in our careers. We can't completely embrace our power if we're not connected to our intuitions because that, along with our unique perspectives, is our power.

One issue is that we're always afraid to put ourselves out there. We're afraid to be ourselves because we're so scared of judgment from others. But what if—instead of fear of judgment from other people—we focus on being our true selves and letting go of the idea that everybody has to like us? There are billions of people in this world. Most of them are not going to like us. It's only important that *you* like you. This is where courage really plays a role.

Courage is feeling the fear and doing it anyway. It's not about feeling scared; it's about what you do with that fear. One of the ways to build self-confidence and self-esteem is by working through those fears so that you can accomplish something challenging. The more we accomplish our goals and handle the events that are difficult in our lives, the better we're going to feel about ourselves. And the better we feel about ourselves, the more willing we are to take action to move through fear.

In terms of work culture, it's really important to foster a supportive and inclusive work environment. Work culture tends to be in the hands of the boss, the CEO, or whoever might be on top of that hierarchy in business. As an employee, it can feel like we don't have the power to influence our work culture. However, anyone in any role can be a *leader*.

There's also a fear of being feminine in the workplace. And there's this stereotypical idea that women need to act like a man would in business. There's a lot of history to that because, in the past, it was always the men who did the heavy lifting. In modern workplaces, societal pressures and unspoken rules persist, and they tell us the "traditional" traits of women—such as collaboration or emotional vulnerability—are harmful to our career advancement. We make conscious or subconscious decisions to behave more "masculine" in order to appear more competent.

What if this old way of believing is actually holding us back? By empowering women to step into their authentic selves, we learn that we don't have to be masculine in order to be powerful. In fact, this idea of acting like a man in our careers puts us in a position where maybe we're aggressive instead of assertive, and we garner less respect, positive regard, and efficiency. As the world of research continues to evolve, we've learned that traditional feminine traits are our greatest strengths. Empathy and compassion breathe life into relationships across the spectrum. The more connected we are with others, the more they feel valued. When people feel and believe they are valued, they will do more and do those things with even more competency. When we filter our intuition through self-limiting beliefs—this idea of needing masculine energy and acting like a man in the workplace—we hold ourselves back. Because our power is in our uniqueness, it's in that gut feeling.

When we, our co-workers, or our employees are experiencing fear, stress, anger, frustration, and irritation, our fight-flight-freeze response lights up. When we are in that state, all access to our frontal lobe (where rational thought, critical thinking and reasoning skills, executive functioning, problem-solving skills, and processing emotion into language) is shut off. How are we supposed to manage conflict, solve problems as they arise, and effectively communicate if we're so disconnected from ourselves, others, and our skills? When we, as women, step fully into ourselves and into a different mindset and set of skills, we're then able to create a better work culture for ourselves and others that nurtures and empowers our employees and coworkers to step into their best selves. When we are able to work as our best selves, we accomplish way more than we were before—even more than we thought could be possible.

The fact is, if we can learn the skills in our mindset perspective, especially within ourselves, we own who we are. We recognize our humanity. And we're aware of our assets and liabilities. We can use our skills and our assets to help us manage our liabilities. We don't have to be at the mercy of the culture that we work in. Our culture at work can either help us grow or help us be scared and get stuck.

There are strategies for creating a balance between work and personal life. When we are working in a harmful work culture environment, we tend to bring that home with us. We tend to come home with nothing left in our tank. We go to bed dreading the next day. We wake up not wanting to go to work and are stressed. We're stuck in this worry mindset because we're afraid of the unknown. We're afraid of what might happen. We're afraid of people repeating their patterns.

Once we learn that how people treat us is not a reflection on us—it's a mirror to themselves and how they see the world based on their mindsets and perspectives—we learn that we don't have to take on that mindset and those feelings as our own. And when we can learn to better manage how we perceive others, we maintain our power. We can manage ourselves so that we don't have to be at the mercy of other people and their baggage. When we can do that, we can start the day by saying, "I'm confident in my skills. I'm confident in conflict resolution. I'm confident in my emotional management. I'm confident in my skills as a worker. And I'm confident that no matter what challenges arise during my day, I have the mental skills to work through them in a way that works for me." When we are able to do that, we get to come home with energy in our tank, which we can use to continue our education. We can use it to run those errands. We can use it to nurture our families and our relationships. We can use that to nurture ourselves. We can go to bed feeling good about the day and how we behaved. Even if we reflect and say, "You know what? I didn't like how I did this." Well, guess what? With the right mindset, that's a growth opportunity. It's not a place to get stuck. It's not a place to ruminate. We don't need to do that. We don't need to beat ourselves up anymore because nothing's wrong with us. And I like to think of every person as a drop of water; just imagine the impact of the ripple effect.

You are just one person, but you can be the catalyst for positive changes in your life within yourself and with loved ones, strangers, and all the people you work with. As one person, shifting your mindset, developing new cognitive skills, and learning how to accept yourself and step into your authentic self can have a tremendous impact on the world, on your community, and on society. When we help that one person, when we are kind to that stranger in line, when we respond with compassion instead of criticism, and when we respond to someone's anger and defensiveness with curiosity, think about how that's going to impact them. How can that lead to more understanding? How can it improve our ability to come together to solve problems?

Imagine what we'd see shift in another person because of how we treated them and conducted ourselves. What if their next step is to be kinder to another person? That's how one person can be so powerful in their environment. That's leadership. Practicing a daily self-appraisal helps us to evaluate our progress. We reflect on our personal and professional actions. We look at the areas where we did things really well and where we did things differently than we normally would have, and we look at the results. We also look at the places where we feel we fell short, where we feel we could have done things differently, and discover how we can apply what we've learned to the future.

When we look at weaknesses and mistakes as opportunities for growth, rather than looking at them as if something's wrong with us, imagine the empowerment that we can feel. If we're committed to doing the next right thing and we discover and uncover the areas where we want to grow more, then we can make different decisions daily and on a moment-to-moment basis. We can make different decisions on how we want to track and engage with our thinking process. We can make different decisions on how we manage the physical sensations of our emotions and how we choose how to respond rather than just react emotionally. We can use self-appraisal to learn more about ourselves and figure out how to apply the skills we've been implementing to the areas where we're already doing well. Then, we can apply them to other areas of life that are where it is apparent that we need or want to change to continue our personal journey. And that piece is important.

Self-improvement is a lifelong journey, which sounds overwhelming. When we look at it as a journey, we can break it down into a series of events. When we can break it down into a series of events and we can be mindful about it, then we're able to make changes. We cannot create change by obsessing over the past or worrying about the future. The only way we can implement change is in the present moment. It's the next decision that we make. It's how we manage ourselves in this moment, in this interaction, during this event. When we try to be on a quest for perfection, we set ourselves up for failure because we're not allowing ourselves to be human.

We keep coming back to this idea of humanity, that we are fallible. Mistakes are a part of life. They are normal, and they are to be expected.

To tie all of this to work culture, when it demands perfection, we will always fall short. We lose our self-confidence, we lose our self-esteem, we are self-critical, we berate ourselves, and we become fearful of making mistakes. This takes us out of the present moment, which means we're going to make more mistakes, which means we're going to get more criticism from whoever's in charge and from other employees. See how our mindset can really make or break how we feel about ourselves? These feelings impact our abilities to apply skills and to step into the person we are deep down as well as the person we want to be.

We also have to be careful that we're not comparing ourselves to other people. We tend to compare our inner world to somebody else's presentation of themselves. And we know from our own experiences of masking ourselves—putting on a different face in different environments—that how we present ourselves and how we think and feel about ourselves internally don't always line up. If we can recognize that the only person we need to compare ourselves to is the person we were an hour ago, or yesterday, or last week, or three months ago, or a year ago, then we can focus on those incremental periods and aspects of growth without the self-criticism because we're accepting all parts of ourselves. When we can focus on those incremental pieces of growth, starting with a single decision, then we can celebrate ourselves. As women, we have exceedingly high expectations of ourselves. We believe we have more to prove so when we accomplish the small things, we don't always look at them and feel good about them because they're merely a means to an end.

But what if the right way to see growth—the way that's going to be most effective long term—is by celebrating the bite-sized wins? Because if we can do it once, we can do it in the next moment. We can do it again in an hour. We can do it tomorrow.

If we're not celebrating ourselves every step of the way, then even when we reach a goal, it's not going to be fulfilling. It's not going to feel good enough because we're not recognizing the power and the courage it takes from moment to moment to focus on doing things differently. It takes a lot of strength and fortitude to evaluate ourselves honestly. We want to shift our mindset from evaluating ourselves in terms of comparing ourselves to other people to evaluating ourselves for ourselves. Personal growth and development is a really hard thing to do, which is why a lot of people don't do it. Many people cannot look at themselves honestly and accept themselves as they are because they have so many core beliefs they are afraid to challenge. They're afraid of who they are underneath those core beliefs. Because there's this fear of, "Oh my gosh, if I recognize and I learn that this whole time, I've been the one in my own way," we end up in this mindset of, "Well, what if? What if I had figured this out earlier? What if I had done this differently? Where would I be right now? We need to learn that "what ifs" are based on fear, criticism, and judgment.

The fact is, we all do the best we can with what we have available to us at that moment. And that's why celebrating those individual moments is so important. We want to make sure that we are present and mindful because when we're aware of the moments, we get to experience the fullness of life. There's beauty in the mundane. There's beauty in sitting and watching a movie with our families. There's beauty in our commute to work. There's gratitude. There's love, there's kindness, there's compassion, and there's empathy. And those things start with us. Because how we behave and how we treat other people is a reflection of us.

If we want to live our lives differently, we need to adapt ourselves from the inside out. We need to build ourselves up and make changes from the inside out because, again, how we think about ourselves, how we feel about the world, the way we perceive ourselves and other people, and the way we talk to ourselves will influence our personal and professional lives.

The longest relationship we will ever have is with ourselves. Reflect on that for a moment. We should be our own best friends, and yet we are our own harshest critics. Think about living our lives through self-criticism, beratement, or self-judgment. What kind of life is that going to create? How is that life going to feel? What kind of relationship are you building with yourself? The way we interact with the world is a reflection of how we see and treat ourselves.

I ask my clients all the time: If a friend of yours came to you and expressed their inner fears, their inner dialogue, and their self-criticism, how would you respond to them? I bet you would not talk to your friend or a loved one the way you talk to yourself. We need to be our own best friends. We need to be our own first loves. One of the tips that I provide people is to let your inner dialogue be friend to friend, not between enemies. When we can be our own friends and we can nurture our own relationship with ourselves, man, life feels damn good. It's not how our lives look that matters, even though that's what society says. It's how our lives *feel* that makes us whole.

We're learning now, as a society, that the number one impact on our overall well-being is our mindset. It's perspective. It's our relationship with ourselves. It's about being emotionally connected. It's about having acceptance. It's about loving ourselves as we are in this moment. That's what matters. How does your life feel? How do you want to feel? Together, we can bridge that gap.

You are enough. You're more than enough. You're *you*. You're a woman—strong, powerful, resilient, and a natural leader. You're unique. It's your uniqueness that really defines who you are. Tap into your authentic self and stop living by societal expectations or the expectations of people who don't really have a say in your life. And even if they do, take everything they say and run it through a filter of your values; hold on to what helps you, work through what's triggering areas where you want to grow, and discard the rest. When we're not carrying that excess baggage, we create an improved reality for ourselves.

We open ourselves up to possibilities and opportunities that never seemed possible or that were never even on our radar. I've learned that every rock-bottom experience has a trapdoor if we keep digging. And that's what we tend to do. We dig ourselves deeper and deeper. And we find ourselves in this deep, dark hole all alone. But what if not only do bottoms have trap doors, but what if tops have trap ceilings? What if every step we take brings us closer and closer to a goal that we never thought possible for ourselves? And what happens? What could happen if we reach that ceiling? It doesn't mean we're done. Maybe we will take a break. But at some point, we're going to stand up and say, "You know what? I heard something above me. Let me push on the ceiling tile."

So keep going. There is no end to personal growth and development. There is no such thing as perfection. There is no ultimate goal, no feeling of completion. There is no end to our journey.

We are simply building a fulfilling life where our jobs and careers are a part of our lives, but they don't have to be the end-all-be-all. And they don't have to create chaos for the rest of our lives. We can find balance. We can put ourselves first in a healthy way. I've learned that selfishness has a really negative connotation. However, there's a difference between being selfish and being self-obsessed. There's a difference between being selfish and harming other people. We're taught at a young age that being selfish is wrong.

But what if *they* were wrong? What if being selfish means putting yourself first? Because when we can put ourselves first in our own lives, we have a very full cup, and we can pour some good stuff into other people. And the cool thing is that when givers meet up with givers, our cups overflow. And look at that trickle-down effect.

There's a question I ask clients: If you're walking down the street with a cup of coffee and someone bumps into you and you spill your coffee, why did you spill your coffee? Everyone will say, "Because someone bumped into me." Well, how about this? You spilled your coffee because coffee was in your cup. If it was water, you'd spill water. Same if it was juice, or milk, or acid… The message here is that life is going to bump into you as you move through it. When it does, what's going to spill out is whatever you're carrying. It could be anger, blaming, judgmentalness, criticism, or violence. It could also be love, kindness, compassion, empathy, understanding, acceptance, and the ability to not take things personally. What do you want to have spilled? What is the legacy you want to leave behind? What evidence of your existence do you want trickled down to others and future generations?

Leadership is not a title. It's how we empower and encourage those around us to step into their best selves and do *their* best work. Leadership is how we conduct and carry ourselves and how we treat ourselves and others. It's about intention and impact. Leadership is how we make others *feel*. As an effective leader, we create space for those around us to grow; we collaborate to allow them to feel their own competence and confidence. Are the people around you growing, happy, confident, and collaborative? If so, you are a true leader.

My hope for anyone impacted by reading this is that you will look for support. Look for a mentor. Look for a coach. Look for people who have the internal life that you want. If you want what they have, we need to learn how they do it. We want people we respect as human beings. Not because they have a certain title, a big house, a vacation home, or a Porsche. It doesn't matter. Those material things don't matter. At the end of the day, those things—the stuff, the jobs, the careers—can come and go in a heartbeat. But we are lasting. Our impact on others is lasting.

I have learned through over a decade of being a licensed therapist, with the plethora of my experiences going through my own personal journey—struggles, harsh truths, and learning new skills—that the things I've presented here are possible for anyone who wants them. I have the honor and privilege of saying I have helped countless women reach new heights from the inside out. This change is completely attainable for all people who have the desire, open-mindedness, and willingness to put in the work. To face fears. To make changes.

Take back your power so that you can change your own life. When we change our internal lives for the better, we change everything around us, and life starts to look more and more beautiful every day.

If you want to go deeper into how to change and adapt and create a growth mindset in your life, reach out. Let's talk one-on-one about your personal story, your journey, and your goals. You can ask me anything. Let's see how we can work together so you can build a life that feels great, where you can learn to ride the wave of life without it drowning you. We learn to go with the flow and surf that wave. We become more flexible and adaptable and develop those personal skills so that you can succeed in all areas of your life beyond your wildest dreams.

∼

Marissa Yubas is a licensed therapist, mindset expert, and transformation coach dedicated to helping individuals achieve inner peace and fulfillment through her practice, Thriving Mind Coaching. Marissa integrates her personal journey, formal education, and clinical expertise to guide clients toward meaningful, lasting change and personal growth.

As a pioneer in the mental wellness space, she is actively involved in the development of InPower, an upcoming social media app designed to foster meaningful connections through emotional intelligence, effective communication, and psychoeducation. Marissa is a featured guest on numerous podcasts and regularly speaks at events and conferences.

Marissa is also an executive contributor for *Brainz Magazine*, where she shares insights and practical strategies for enhancing mental well-being and overall quality of life. A firm believer in the power of personal narratives, she encourages others to embrace their unique stories as a source of strength and inspiration.

To connect with Marissa,
follow her on
Instagram @marissayubasmft

or reach out via email at
marisayubasmft@gmail.com.

Beyond the Racquet

BY TASHA DOUCAS

The purpose of this chapter is to inspire those to try the game of squash and for clubs to consider investing in squash courts, knowing how this sport promotes good health, engagement, personal resilience, and connection. This sport is like no other!

It creates a community, a close-knit family of those who enjoy the sport—players of all ages and backgrounds come together through sport and support each other through the game. It builds a healthy body and mind. And it provides many life lessons.

Why should you listen to a woman who grew up in a very male-dominated sport in the French Canadian city of Montreal? Well, I struggled to overcome countless setbacks, yet at the time, I didn't see them as setbacks; I saw them as doors of opportunity to be opened. I was a girl who never really understood the word NO. My parents said it often enough throughout my childhood, however, I feel it gave me the creativity to figure a way around the no's and get to the end point I was focused on. I have utilized that creativity throughout my life to help me strive to where I felt I needed to be at the time, with the level of impact, contribution, and self-development at each stage I was in. Squash has done this for me, and the lessons I have learned along the way have impacted all aspects of my life, through my career, parenthood, managing my health, my community contributions through volunteerism and mentorship... essentially leadership of my life. I want others to benefit from these lessons to overcome obstacles in their life and be the leader that they know and strive to be.

At age 13, squash was my playing ground to learn resilience, patience, perseverance, setting goals, determination, focus, visualization, and community. All the skills that have built the foundation of leadership, value, purpose, and passion during my life. The Squash community, as a whole, has shaped me into the person I am today: a passionate and thoughtful coach motivating new players to share and experience the same joys and life lessons that I've experienced throughout my life.

My hope is that you will be inspired to find a squash court near you and build a community that provides the support to fuel your life like it has for me. And if you have any challenges finding one, there are plenty of national or local organizations, depending on where you live, that can help you find one, such as:

- Squash Canada
- US Squash
- England Squash
- Egyptian Squash
- Squash Australia

For those who currently play, I hope you realize how special this sport is, and that you continue to share the joy of the game with others and contribute your time to your local organization.

Drive Your Goals Through Mindset

The underlying foundation of anything we achieve is mindset, hence why I start this chapter with this learned skill. We hear everybody talking about it: *"You have to have the right mindset in order to do x, y, and z."* Well, firstly, what exactly is mindset? Merriam-Webster's

Dictionary states that mindset is a mental attitude or a state of mind. At the end of the day, everybody has their own definition, however brief or complex. My definition is how we prime our minds for the things we want to achieve. Some may call this faith or others, intention.

A couple of years ago, I hired a coach to work with my son daily on executive functioning and routines. One day, the topic of discussion was mindset: a *fixed* versus *growth* mindset. I was curious, so I read through the documents to better understand what exactly they meant by it. And now, because I'm aware of it, I see the term growth mindset everywhere.

A fixed mindset means that everything stays the way it is and doesn't evolve—you kind of put yourself in this box. Would you want to stay in that box, especially if there is no room to bend the lines of that box? As for a growth mindset, it's about seeing that the life lessons you go through are all working towards your growth as an individual human being. It's not about getting things perfect the first time; it's more about how you learn and the journey you are on. How do you grow as a person through that journey? How do you push some of the boundaries of that box so you don't feel trapped in a confined area?

As a kid, my mindset was always one of curiosity, exploration, and self discovery. Somehow every time I was faced with a challenge, I knew that there were other ways around it; I knew that it was a kind of fork in the road that I got to figure out which way I should travel at that time. I barely spent a second thinking *I'm not good enough. I can't do it. I don't have the time.* All these were excuses to me that didn't serve me. And then I would see the path; *Down that road, at the end of that road, that's what I want. That's what I'm gonna go for and I'm gonna do it!*

In anything we do—and especially in sports—it's the vision, it's the goal that drives everything that we do, whether it's winning a match, winning a local competition, a National Championship or even a World Class event. The journey toward the end of that road can be long, but we don't have to see it that way. We can choose to see it as *just getting on the road and driving*. And when we get to the next pit stop, we realize we've learned something new, and we can bring it with us, continue driving, and carry on.

On the Squash court, that vision created a mindset of focus, positivity, encouragement, consistency, and drive. Every day during drills, whether it be running drills or technical drills, I was always hungry to improve, whether beating my running times or getting the ball straighter and closer to the wall. Seeing that improvement, whether small or by leaps, had me wanting to do more for the next stage. Then, when it came to match time, I would use that as a way to test out my speed, agility, and accuracy on the court. Any game or match lost was not a devastation; it was a sense of clarity on what elements needed my focus next, and then once I worked on those areas, I would test it again through match or tournament play.

Life gets to be like that: Learn something new, practice at it, and if some elements fail, then learn from it, tweak the process, and then test it out again.

I see mindset as the muscle that continues to develop, grow, and become more defined.

If you've ever worked out or lifted weights before, you know you need to build muscle uniformly. If you start with bicep curls, you'll need to do triceps next to balance out the muscles in your arm. And you wake up every day and do it because you know that repetition and consistency will help develop strength, and then it becomes a habit. It's your mindset that drives you towards your goal.

My Story

I started playing tennis at the age of seven, and it became all I wanted to do. Nothing else gave me such joy. I watched my older siblings head to the tennis court all the time, particularly in the summer when school was out. I wanted to be part of the action. I wanted to move. My body *needed* to move every morning. So I'd wake up, eat breakfast, and ride a 10-minute bike route to be at the tennis courts for a 9 a.m. program. At that young age, my mom had me return home at lunch. I cried when I had to leave to return home because I loved playing tennis and being with my friends. Once I got a little bit older, I was allowed to return to the courts in the afternoon. A few years later, when my mom felt it was okay for me to ride my bike home in the evenings, I would go out there and play after dinner and come back home in the pitch dark once the courts closed for the night. I am not sure what exactly my fixation was about always being on the tennis court. But you know what? It was so much fun because I was able to be outside and play all day. I got to play with different people and make friends. It was my little community.

With so many hours on the court, I knew that I was building muscle as well as memory muscle in preparation for something that I wasn't quite sure what it was for just yet. I just knew that I had to keep going, hitting that ball, serving that ball, and running towards that ball. I was always meeting different people at the club, from other kids my age and friends of my siblings or my Dad. As I got older and better, I would then be paired up to play against adults in singles as well as doubles play and eventually learned various strategies and tactics along the way. I didn't really have any intention about the actual development of the strategic part of the game; I just loved learning and figuring out how I could improve my game and win the next point, the next game, and then the match.

Reflecting back, yes, there was that aspect of competition that I found thrilling and still do to this day. I sometimes will use Squash tournaments to challenge my athleticism and the psychology of gameplay to test myself. At the time, as a kid, I also think it was being around people who enjoyed the same thing—a sense of community —that kept me coming back. I watched my dad over the years build his communities with his soccer league team that he established with other dads who immigrated to Canada. They were from all over the world: Germany, Holland, Hungary, Mexico, Spain, France, etc. That community, along with their families, gathered every few months at someone's house to socialize, play a fun game of soccer, share in food and drink, and connect. He also built his community at the local outdoor tennis courts and then soon after with the Squash community. Being President of the Montreal Amateur Athletic Association in Montreal for a few years in the '80s, becoming a Jester advocating for Squash (thejestersclub.org), and traveling for tournaments where he would connect with friends, go out for dinner, and enjoy the thrill of a competitive match were all elements for him of being in community with like-minded individuals.

By the age of 13, my family was a member of the Montreal Amateur Athletic Association (now ClubSportifMAA) in Montreal, Quebec, which has an incredibly rich history of Olympic-level swimmers, track and field competitors, as well as Football Grey Cup and Hockey Stanley Cup legends. There was no other club with this level of inspiration for greatness in Canada at the time. My siblings were playing squash or badminton, so I decided to give squash a go. With my background in tennis and already having good hand-eye coordination, I had an affinity towards hitting the fast-paced ball of Squash. I L-O-V-E-D it!

In my home life, however, I felt really stuck. It wasn't the environment I wanted to spend my teenage years hanging out in. I was unhappy. I felt trapped. I wanted more out of my life outside the confines of our house walls. I wanted to have a happy life—a life that I saw out there in the world, and saw the opportunity to play squash competitively. Being the last of four kids, and watching my siblings playing racquet sports, and being taxi'd by my parents to their tournaments, I could see myself traveling for tournaments as well. Getting to meet new people and spend time away from home was a thought that really excited me. One thing I didn't realize at the time is that Squash would give me a way to develop my emotional intelligence: being able to better manage my emotions that started exploding in my teenage years.

The next few years were the highlight of my life, traveling, playing squash, and having a refuge away from a life of rigidity filled with lots of no's said to me and restrictiveness in my schedule. I would relive the highs of my squash moments in a heartbeat!

At the age of 18, my life took a huge turn when the local police showed up at our home unexpectedly. They came to inform us that my older brother passed away in a tragic boating accident. His family, friends, and squash acquaintances were completely stunned. Everybody liked him so much! And to this day, each story I hear about him from people is unique and filled with his joy of squash, being so present in moments with friends, essentially the joy of life! His raw talent from juniors had gotten him accepted on a full squash scholarship to Harvard, however, he decided to turn professional and go on tour. By age 24, his professional squash career continued to soar, and he had just become the rookie of the year in the North American hardball doubles squash circuit. My brother was my idol—the person I looked up to. He's the reason I started playing squash: I saw the possibility of escaping my drab home life. In a way, I felt I was following in his footsteps, and now, that connection was gone. Not only was my brother gone, but I felt the reason I'd been competing and traveling for Squash for the last five years was gone, too; I felt my purpose had disintegrated in a moment.

With any death, there's a period where you feel like there's a dark cloud above you or a piece of your heart that's missing, and you're trying to figure out what you can do about it. I remember telling my mom, "You know what? It just doesn't feel real. It feels like he moved to some other country." I realize this thinking may sound weird, but we tend to come up with these kinds of stories to give ourselves comfort. I remember getting on the squash court, and for months, I wouldn't be able to hit the ball with purpose. I tanked my tournament matches into quick losses until I started coming out of my dark cloud. Eventually, I started getting back to playing again for the joy of it. One day, when I returned home after a tournament, my mom made some passive-aggressive comment criticizing me and asking if I was ever gonna amount to anything and get better results. Her comment triggered me so much that I went to my room, and in that moment, I thought, *You know what? She's right.* I didn't want to be getting the same results over and over again. That's when I responded to her... in my head... *I'll show you!*

At that time, I was ranked 8th in Canada in the under-19s for singles squash. I gave myself three months to improve my ranking to number 5 in Canada, and I had to figure out how. *Well, what is the formula that would get me there?* I had a certain number of tournaments left to play in the season that would impact my ranking, and I had very little time to work with. So I said to myself, *Okay, there's going to be a few things I need to change in order to get the result I want.*

1. Increase my training regimen
2. Add meditation to the equation.
3. Better preparation and warmup ahead of my matches.

For the first change, every morning I would wake up early and head to the club before school to run drills and then return after school to drill again and play matches.

Secondly, for the meditation, I used mental visualization. I had just recently watched a documentary with Michael Jordan talking about the time he got quite injured and couldn't play basketball for several months, however, by practicing daily mental visualization, he came back to playing at the same level as just before he had gotten injured. It got me curious, so I learned to visualize at night, followed by listening to a relaxation tape made by my coach to help my body get into deep sleep and recovery. The third change was preparation on the day of my matches. I reflected on how I felt previously: *Ya know, I seem to get into my game too late. By the time I turn on the engine to play well, the match is already done,* and I realized that I hadn't really gotten a good sweat on, and what would make a difference is getting really warmed up and getting a sweat going prior to stepping on court to play my match.

So, I developed a routine covering all three aspects. Some things worked; some things didn't. As an example, when I started visualizing, I would first visualize myself running drills and then it would evolve to playing a match in my head. The first couple of times I did it, I'd be hitting these amazing shots. I'd think, *Oh, I'm just gonna play a great shot every single time; that's how I wanna show up on court.* And then, when my opponents in the actual tournament match managed to get the ball back after what I thought was a perfect shot, I just completely froze and lost the match. So then I thought, *Okay, let's tweak this. Let me play four games in my head, and let me make some rallies last a little longer.* Well, I started seeing results, yet I still needed to make some tweaks. In my visualization practice, I worked my way up to playing five-game matches with very long rallies. When I got to actual matches, and even for those that had very long rallies, I didn't feel as exhausted as I would have previously, as my mental preparation prepared me for the cardio as well. I'd think I can do this. *I can get through this.* And to think that when I started this meditation process, it was so hard just to close my eyes and think about it for a mere 60 seconds. However, when I got into a daily routine and sometimes did it twice in a day to build up consistency and intensity, I was able to get to at least 40 minutes. I put in the practice, put in the work, and I put in the focus on my body. I'd ensure I could recover, and then I'd do this visualization. And all the while, my mindset was that I would never give up; even when I felt like, *Oh, my God, this is tough. Can I really do this? I'm tired! I don't want to meditate.* I said, Hey, you have three months to make it happen. Do it! *It's a small sacrifice that I have to pay to reach my goals and end my junior division on a high note.* And you know what? I did! Three months later, after setting my goal, I had done exactly what I set out to do; I increased my ranking by 3 points, and I finished my junior singles career at number 5 in Canada.

Mindset is everything, and aligning it with your goals and establishing a consistent routine makes all the difference in helping you accomplish what you set out to do. If you want something bad enough and are willing to put the effort in, you can do it. And you know what? When there are tough days, you just push through it. You get it done and say, "I FEEL good." It feels good to stick to a plan, push yourself, and get it done because you're holding yourself accountable for your results, and you show up as a leader. A leader, in this case, over myself and accomplishing a massive goal I set out to achieve. Going forward, I felt like I could achieve anything following this mindset, dedication, and perseverance. I felt LIMITLESS!

Accelerate Your Results With Self-Awareness

Self-awareness is a critical tool to accelerate your growth in whatever you want to improve.

Being on a coaching path at this stage in my life, my method of coaching squash is about creating space for my students, whatever age they are, to self-reflect on the results they're getting and what is impacting those results. One of my regular sayings is, "The ball will always give you the feedback you need." It all depends on what you learn from where the ball lands after you hit the ball. Does it land short? Does it land deep? Does it land close to the wall? Does it land in the middle of the court? Does it bounce off the sidewall before hitting the front wall? Does it hit the front wall and then hit the side wall? The ball provides feedback based on a few factors:

- Be aware of the angle your body is facing. Is it facing the side wall or not?
- Where are you making contact with the ball? Are you in front of the ball or behind the ball?
- Are you watching the ball? Are you watching the ball make contact with the strings of your racquet?

And it goes further from what the ball is saying to you, asking yourself, *How is my body feeling when I am hitting a shot? Am I focused on hitting length for every single shot I make? Am I making it difficult for myself to hit an impossible shot?* For example, are you really reaching for the ball and struggling to hit it to go deep, however, it falls short in the middle of the court where your opponent can attack it with a winner, as opposed to hitting a drop shot because it takes less effort yet is still effective?

Sometimes, we make it so hard on ourselves when we can actually make it easier on ourselves and achieve a much better result. It's about being open to listening to our bodies and our thoughts, assessing the situations, and figuring out the right approach in that type of situation. It's not about one shot or one approach that will win the rally or help us overcome an obstacle every time.

Paying attention to the situation, where the other player is, and how easy it is for you to get to the ball will help you determine the right approach. And if it doesn't work, then making small yet effective tweaks to accomplish what you set out to do is all about self-awareness and responding to it in the moment. It's important to adapt, not only between games but even during a game when you are losing a few rallies in a row. That's self-awareness. Sometimes, it's called being laser-focused on the court where you are watching that ball like there's nothing else going on in that court.

The other aspect of being tuned in to self-awareness is the self-talk piece. We hear people say, "You know, you shouldn't talk bad to yourself. You gotta be positive and optimistic!" Sometimes, it feels forced. But the words we use are so important. They impact how we see ourselves, and that sets up how we respond to situations. "My backhand sucks," which I hear often, is our own perception, whether we have learned it from others saying that backhand is a more difficult shot to make or maybe we haven't practiced it as much as our forehand. There are caveats to both of those shots in Squash. We just have to be self-aware of how we hit each of those shots. The forehand is just as easy to mess up, particularly if our bodies are facing the front wall as opposed to the side wall, for instance. When I help my students use phrases such as "My backhand is improving each time I practice getting behind the ball and using control," or "Slowing down my racquet swing is giving me more accuracy and consistency," they start seeing results, and it gets to be easy to hit the ball with length.

Positive self-talk allows us to be more open to feedback and become more self-aware of the reality of the situation. This, in turn, allows us to make better and more effective decisions. This holds true in real life, whether in our careers, our relationships, etc.

Executing a Vision With Intentional Focus

In order to create the discipline to drive through to execution, your vision needs to be big, have real meaning, and have an intended impact. The clearer the goals, the easier it is to execute.

And when it comes to impact, it helps to determine how committed you are. When thinking about a goal, say the words: "I am committed. I am ready to..." followed by each of your specific and targeted goals.

This intentional focus comes over you; it embodies you. You want this so much that you are willing to do what it takes to reach that goal. That commitment creates the intention and focus for you to actually execute on the steps to get there. I find that discipline becomes easier to incorporate, and habit-building becomes easier to implement because you have this larger inner purpose driving you to do the work.

Coming back to my squash story, I was very clear on my vision: My goal was to increase my national ranking by three points in a very short time. I made that commitment to myself with great intention, great clarity, and great focus. When I laid out the steps that I needed to take to get to my goal, the execution part became easy. "Tell me what I have to do," and that vision carried me every day. From waking up early to get on the bus to the squash courts so I could do drills to the days when it was cold outside or snowy, I still got up and took the bus to the club. What that intention did was get me out the door at 6:30 in the morning; the rest was done on autopilot.

For the past eight months at the time of writing this story, I've been working as a paid Assistant Squash Professional at my club, Vancouver Lawn Tennis & Badminton Club. Two years ago, as I was shifting away from my corporate career and coming off of chairing a board of my provincial squash association, I wanted to dive further into the need to grow female participation and female coaches. The fire in me to want to impact these numbers grew and grew, and I finally committed wholeheartedly to this mission. I determined the coaching courses I needed to complete on this path to becoming an accredited squash coach and completed a series of instructor courses with a fast-track focus.

I got to the next step and started building out a plan for how I could consult with various clubs on how they could grow their female participation rates and build more squash engagement for their facility. At my club, I volunteered every Wednesday for nine months to provide coaching tips for the ladies in the drop-in session. That was every week for a good part of a year, showing up and engaging with ladies, practicing my coaching skills, and seeing what worked to help these ladies improve. I knew that if I presented things in a way that required only small changes to see great improvement, that would be a concept that was easily digestible for my audience. If there are big changes required in order to see wins, that can often become overwhelming. However, if you can implement small tweaks in order to have a serious and productive impact on your game then it becomes more doable, more encouraging, and more fun.

When the Head Pro and the Club Administration gave me the opportunity as a Squash Coach and it was announced that there was a dedicated female coach to help engage and work with the ladies, the participation numbers rapidly grew, and we are now more than triple those numbers. There is a true need and desire for a space that creates a sense of belonging, support, learning, and fun for women. Every six to eight weeks, we host a "Squash and Sip" event, and it is a true celebration of women coming out and having fun connecting with other women while playing squash and now all of our courts are used to capacity!

Watching these ladies take over the squash courts with laughter while getting exercise and working on their game, I see the passion that I've had all these years being adopted by so many others, it fuels me to ask, "How can we do more of this on a wider scale? How can we create this in other clubs?" I've found women who have the same desire as I do to create squash-playing communities. From my eyes, it's such a beautiful way to empower women to speak their voice, and get involved in growing a community.

The Power of Mentorship

Becoming a limitless leader does not happen overnight, and it does not happen alone. It's a journey done in a community! The experiences that we have and the people we meet impact us in one way or another. They guide us in shaping who we are and who we get to become.

Mentorship is a key element on this journey toward becoming a leader. There are times when we are being mentored without even realizing it. You may not have established a plan or thought through the outcomes. Yet, here you are, recalling all the people who have crossed your path and were mentoring you, essentially helping you shape your way of leadership.

Reflecting on my past, I've had a good number of people who have mentored me. Let's put it this way: Coaches in my sport didn't always have an official title as coach. However, they were there at the time that I was ready to listen and implement their guidance, and they were able to shape it in a way that allowed me to execute more effectively.

There are others who may have simply given me one sentence of advice that was so instrumental to help me effect change on the path I was on. One time I recall when I was learning to play hardball doubles squash in my early 30s, and I decided to play a professional/amateur event where a professional doubles player pairs up with an amateur player to play against another team on the same court.

My partner told me that in order to win doubles, the match is won by placing the ball deep in the back of the court. The reality is that to put your partner on the defense and cough up a loose shot for you to hit it short, you must first hit it deep in the back of the court. If I look back on my doubles career for the last 20 years, most of my winning shots were with a high lob, floating to the back, dropping straight onto the ground before the back wall, and dying. That lesson I take into my squash coaching now, whether it's singles or doubles. It was one line that spoke volumes and made strategy incredibly easy for me to implement as well as teach others. In order to allow these words of wisdom to take shape, it's in that when I got this advice, I was open. My mind and heart were open to receive, and that allowed me to keep this as a guiding principle.

It may seem like a simple thing, but sometimes the best advice that we get is in those simple moments when we are open to receiving.

At the same time, there is an aspect of clarity that helps you align the moment of advice received to match your goals. In this instance, I felt like a 13-year-old girl again, hungry to learn the sport, hungry to improve quickly, and that was my goal. And I had with me the joy of playing a sport that my older brother, my idol, used to play, and playing at a high level with these professional athletes made me feel much closer to him.

The combination of clarity and joy for learning prepares you for mentorship and accelerates your progress even more quickly.

In business, you know you're in the right field, industry, or job when you have a joy for learning, a joy for figuring things out, and a joy for wanting to take it to the next level. I had that in my corporate world for a few periods in my life, and now that I'm an entrepreneur, I get to own all aspects of my priming, my vision, my clarity, and mentorship. No one is going to give it to you on a silver platter; it's something that you seek because you're goal-driven, because you want more, and because it has great meaning to you.

How Do We Receive Feedback and Are We Coachable?

I learned a valuable lesson during a fantastic leadership course I took a few years ago: Feedback is neutral. What a novel idea it was for me at the time. I think I learned from a strict family upbringing that feedback was always something I needed to defend myself from. I always felt on the defensive. Learning this new concept for me was so liberating! Yes, I still have moments where I feel the need to defend myself; however, now I get to experience feedback in a different way that allows me to make choices and see if they align with, first and foremost, my values and beliefs, and secondly, my objectives and my goals for my business in coaching or consultancy.

In my opinion, a good mentor is not necessarily going to be celebrating every win. You have a mentor to help you see what you're not seeing, to help you look in the mirror at certain things, to try to come up with the best solution or approach at that moment, or figure out how to resolve a challenge because they have been there before. This approach helps you become a better leader!

What is your definition of feedback? Can you see feedback as neutral to help propel you forward to become the leader you are destined to be?

The Strength of Collaboration

Collaboration is another key lesson I have learned from at an early age and continue to learn from. When competing in sports as a young athlete, you have to coordinate a schedule with your busy working parents when it comes to driving you to and from school and your training sessions.

Also, you are working with your coach on establishing goals and exercises to work through to improve and see results in your match play. Not all exercises are fun all the time, so you both have to collaborate on what will work from week to week and how you can continue to be engaged in your progress.

In business, there is always collaboration working towards common goals. It's working together to overcome challenges, find long-lasting solutions or come together to expand on messaging to a wider audience. And when it's time to celebrate wins, it's ensuring everyone is involved.

Collaborating within a community fosters a sense of belonging and inspires team members to engage more with one another. The best example I've seen in action is charitable and not-for-profit organizations, with their boards of volunteers who have different perspectives but come together with staff to meet the demands of their organization, with limited resources and minimal time to execute.

Oftentimes in these situations, volunteer directors will jump in to help out where they can. When inspired, stronger engagement is fostered, and a deeper sense of belonging in that community is cultivated.

During my time as board chair of Squash BC, our provincial sports organization, my approach was to listen to the members, the staff, and the board of directors. I was assessing what they had in common, identifying potential gaps of knowledge and alignment, and bringing those forward in our meetings for discussion. Oftentimes, it takes a few different people as well as different discussions to work towards an objective or even a common understanding in order to put a plan together.

One of the communities I'm most proud to be involved with is the Jesters Club. Founded in England in 1929, they are a group who advocates for a few racket sports—namely squash—and who compete in a sportsmanlike manner. The group supports the growth of the game through organized events, volunteering, providing financial support, and partnering with their state, provincial, or federal sports organizations, joining together to create opportunities for those who otherwise might never have had access to squash. It is now a worldwide club of over 3,000 members with branches in Canada, the U.S., South Africa, and Australia.

In the fall of 2022, during the 100th Lapham Grant invitational event between the U.S. and Canada, there was a roundtable discussion with representatives from across Canada, the U.S., and South Africa to discuss ways to grow the sport and how we can continue to learn from each other. We were inspired by each other's passion to grow the sport in our respective regional areas, and we have continued to share so that we can continue to grow collectively.

Creating the opportunity to bring together diverse perspectives enhances overall objectives and leading change through collective contribution that has a positive ripple effect for the future.

Navigating Contrasting Dynamics to Explore Opportunity

Now we get into a juicy topic: contrasting dynamics. This is something I think I was born into. Raised by an Italian mother and a Greek father with French ancestry, fiery comments were always flying around in my household. And being the last of four kids when the first two are 12/13 years older, I had a lot of orders barked at me whether I agreed with them or not. To this day, I still feel that way at certain times.

After years of tennis before adding squash to my sports repertoire, I realized being a girl who played squash in Montreal was very rare. Jordana was the only other girl who was playing competitively, and she was at a higher level of skill than I was. So, as I worked through developing my skills, I played with the boys. Those days, boys could not stand to lose against a girl. It was a total embarrassment for them. So, at the end of each match, I would learn to quickly duck before the racket, and the goggles came flying off and were flown across the court! Being a girl in sport was tough, let alone in the squash community, since not many people knew about or played the game. None of my friends at school really understood what I was doing after school each day and why I couldn't join their social activities on the weekend because of my tournaments.

In those days I found I didn't necessarily fit into some of the social groups. However, when I met friends at the sports club, I found boys who I would hang out with and socialize with. They were my crew, and I knew I could count on them for support.

During my teenage years, I didn't really think about this lack of girls playing in the sport. All I knew was I wanted to play squash, and so I played with the boys; that was it.

When I got into the workforce in my twenties, I started seeing how power at certain levels of leadership was used to manipulate others or the situation. Early on, I had a situation where I was promoted three times in the space of only a few months. Not even a year into my executive assistant role, my boss made the decision to move me to a new department in a completely different building across town. There was no explanation, not even from the contract HR representative who had the audacity to ask me if anything inappropriate had happened with my boss. I was gobsmacked. *What kind of world am I entering here?* I asked myself.

Just like when I was a little girl, I learned to follow orders. I moved to the new position to keep my job and be able to pay rent. A couple of months later, I applied for a position to return to the office. My former colleagues couldn't understand why I had to go through the trouble of interviewing for the job, seeing that I understood the business fairly well. Outside those four white walls, I could hear my former boss whistling in the background. I told my former colleagues at that moment, *"Hear that whistling? That's why I can't come back."* And I proceeded to tell them, *"Call me when he's left the organization so I can reapply."* Then I walked out.

Within a few months after he took his payout, I returned and then worked through a few promotions over the next few years. Upon reflection, I think my competitive squash journey trained me well for my journey with my corporate career—being patient, seeing the bigger picture and developing the strategy that was going to get me where I was striving for, and most of all, not giving up. Keeping my head high, doing the best I could do where I was at, and knowing that if I was consistent, I could persevere and get to the other side of what was waiting for me. Fast forward to the last 20 years, I started working for a law services provider founded and run by women. My eyes opened up to what it was like to have a voice, share product feedback from customers, listen to their needs and concerns, and have a seat at the table, collaborating, strategizing, and implementing the vision of the organization. With some years and experience under my belt, I was involved in building out a job description for my next role. I couldn't imagine being in a position where I could write my own job description! My years at this company turned out to be the most challenging yet satisfying time of my corporate career. When I look back, I think that I was given the space to demonstrate my skills, share my thoughts on strategy, speak at their conferences, and feel valued, and I felt that I could put the ask out for new opportunities and new ideas in order to grow. I am so very grateful for that opportunity!

Working for a not-for-profit sports organization, I learned more about sound governance, diversity, and collaboration. That all comes with discussion—not always easy conversations, but ones that start with *I observed, I witnessed,* or *I heard,* and follow up with *What did you observe or hear from your end?* And then... listening. Creating space to hear other people's perspectives has been so helpful for me in whatever goals I am working toward. When translating this to playing squash as a kid, I used to get frustrated with the official standing on a chair peering over the court wall to make their calls, whether it was awarding a point, a replay, or no replay. Regardless of how I saw the situation on the court, I learned that I needed to respect another perspective of the situation. And now, I teach mini-officiating clinics and educate players on perspective, especially when they have someone reffing their matches.

Shifting into squash coaching the last few years, my focus is to ensure I create a safe space for women and girls to learn squash—a space that has no judgment, fosters learning, and builds self-confidence. I have had women come up to me to tell me how the squash program has given them so much more self-confidence on and off the court. One time, a player shared that they felt overlooked by the group of 20 players, so I took a moment to assess my actions and said that I felt so bad that I didn't see the situation. I quickly pivoted and fostered a situation of shared learning and had the player move to another court of players that would challenge her. I truly believe that a safe space is there for each of us to request, to foster, and to honor.

Discussion, self-education, and the willingness to approach new concepts with an open mind allow me to better navigate challenging dynamics with others, especially during tense situations, whether on or off the Squash court.

Giving Back

Becoming a mentor to someone is and should be considered a privilege. We can always learn from another person, especially when we're primed to receive.

I am a mentor as well as a mentee, and I plan for that to continue for many years. Having a space where you can impart knowledge, experience, and passion is a great source of gratitude. You know, most everything I do nowadays, I think about my actions and how they would impact or help others. When I sign up to do projects, I'm looking at the impact as well. But before I go shouting all the wisdom I can share, I pause and see the right opportunity: where I'm being asked or where I can get permission to offer advice.

A mentor-mentee relationship is reciprocal, and the collaborative process does not flourish without it. I think it's important that we all see the bigger picture in that we are not on this journey all on our own. Yes, we must do the work ourselves. Yet, in order to do that work carefully, thoughtfully, and effectively, there are outside forces that we can pull from and utilize at various levels.

Take the analogy of driving on a highway to a destination miles and miles away. We can't make it to a destination without fuel or charging our car, and we need to do that periodically to keep us going. We can't keep driving a car unless we're fueled and hydrated. So we need to occasionally pull off into the service lane

Then there's maintenance for a car that needs to be done in order to keep all the moving parts working together. And we may want to have some sort of entertainment to keep our minds alert; maybe listen to a podcast or an Audible story. We know our path, and so we plan for how to stay on that path for a long period of time. It's using these external resources as planned, or as needed to keep us moving to the next milestone.

In my junior years of squash, I felt like I was a sponge, absorbing and learning from everything around me. As a teenager, you're growing emotionally, mentally, and physically, and you're trying to adapt to this new shell—a body that is evolving. I was very fortunate to have good role models around me, and mentors who taught me different skills. The technical aspect of how I played squash, the physical aspect to keep me in shape, and being able to last several matches in a tournament by keeping my mind and my emotions in check and not getting too excited or too frustrated with my game or with my opponent. I didn't want to lose a match just because I couldn't manage my emotions. I had those who helped me with recovery and psychological skills for effective competition play.

In my 20s, I was focused on my career, trying to find the roles that I fit in well yet also challenged me. Over those teenage years in squash, I traveled a lot without my parents and learned from all the families I stayed with. Managing my on-court behavior prepared me for the workforce when I got out of the university. It allowed me to test and develop my skills, to play the corporate game.

Understanding what my bosses saw as success and how I could support that allowed me to climb up the corporate ladder, and in my 30s I used that time to get back into squash. I also moved to the other side of the country and shortly found myself on squash committees. First the doubles committee, then a Squash Canada competition committee. My next step was a board of directors position for Squash BC, and soon after, Board Chair.

That was a huge period of growth and leadership for me, coming back into the sport and bringing some of my corporate ideas and lessons, coupled with my experience in sports over the years. I really wanted to give back to the community that was so giving to me in my younger years. I did have different coaches over the years; some with the title of coach and others were friends of my Dad's at the clubs that I played at who mentored me in various ways. I will never forget this, and because of generosity seeing that I had the drive for growth and the passion for the sport, they gave me their time, patience and guidance. I have felt driven to give back by volunteering in committees over the last decade.

Recently, since my son became a teenager, I've been reflecting on what my parents did for me. As a teenager, the youngest of four, a stubborn yet driven teenage girl, I wanted to live life fully, play squash, and travel. I'm so thankful to my parents who established that space for me. For whatever reason, I wasn't able to establish that same space for my son. I know he's on a different path. My hope is that by modeling being an athlete, a volunteer, a coach, and a community builder spanning cities and even countries, he'll figure out a path of his own that is just as fulfilling as the one I found.

Conclusion

This is only part of my story. I have many more to create from here. And I thank you for letting me share these stories with you. Squash has saved my life in countless ways, and it has taught me many valuable lessons that I've carried throughout various aspects of my life. It has shown me to celebrate wins, big and small, and how to work through and overcome challenges, even severe injury and dealing with the passing of loved ones.

For me, squash is one of the best sports out there, not only because of the game and what it does for your brain, for your confidence, and for your overall health, but also its community. The people I've met along the way and the groups I've been involved with are what I really appreciate about the sport, along with my passion for squash that I get to share every single day!

So, let me ask you this: Are you clear on your vision? Whatever that may be—in business, in sport, or in your relationships. Being clear in each of these areas allows you to stop living in the void and start living in the now, being the leader you get to be and seeking out the mentors that have guidance for you.

If you are looking for more inspiration or guidance on being the best leader you can be to achieve your goals, feel free to check out my website and connect with me. I would love to mentor you on whatever journey you are on.

Tasha Doucas is an athlete, entrepreneur, coach, and family caregiver advocate who has built a life centered around resilience, empowerment, and sport. From playing against boys as a young squash player due to a lack of female competitors to becoming a champion for inclusivity in the sport, her journey has been defined by perseverance and passion.

As a high-level competitor, she has achieved national and international squash success and has played a key role in shaping the squash community as a former SQUASH BC President (2018-2023) and as one of the founding committee members of the Women and Girls in Squash Committee to drive female participation and programming in British Columbia.

Tasha is currently coaching and mentoring athletes at all levels as an assistant coach at Vancouver Lawn Tennis & Badminton Club and a Squash BC coach. She is a certified NCCP coach and instructor, trained in SafeSport, Mental Health in Sport, and Sport Nutrition—reinforcing her commitment to athlete well-being and development.

Beyond the court, she is a dedicated Family Caregiver Consultant, working with Provincial Health Services Authority / PHSA (BC Children's & Women's, PHSA Quality & Safety Steering Committee, PHSA BC Cancer and BC Children's Emergency Department) as a Patient and Caregiver Partner to advocate for better healthcare systems for caregivers and patients.

Her guiding principle, Live Life Fully, is not just a mantra—it's how she moves through the world, inspiring others to embrace joy, success, and personal growth.

Connect with Tasha on social media:

LinkedIn
https://www.linkedin.com/in/tashadoucas/

Instagram
https://instagram.com/TashaDoucas

Facebook
https://www.facebook.com/TashaDoucas/

Website
https://www.radicallyresilient.ca/

The Balance Behind the Breakthrough

BY TIA SMITH

"Mommy, I lied to you. I don't have a test tomorrow. I just wanted you to spend time with me."

That was my wake-up call. Her words hit me like a dagger straight to the heart.

My youngest daughter was seven years old when she came to me after dinner one evening, holding a piece of paper in her small hands. She said she needed help studying for a test. I glanced at the paper and recognized it immediately—it was already graded, a test she'd taken the week before. When I reminded her of this, her face crumpled, and tears spilled down her cheeks. That's when she confessed. She didn't need to study at all. She just wanted my attention.

That moment stopped me in my tracks. I realized the unspoken message I'd been sending my two daughters every single day. It was my first role as a manager. I left for work at 6 a.m. before my girls were even out of bed and came home at 6 p.m., exhausted but still tethered to my laptop. I'd answer emails while making dinner, review reports during family meals, and squeeze in more work after tucking them into bed. I thought I was doing it all—being a hard worker, a dedicated parent, and someone they could admire. But in truth, I wasn't fully present anywhere, least of all at home.

My family account and my health account were completely depleted.

That conversation with my daughter was a wake-up call. It forced me to confront the imbalance I had allowed to creep into my life. I knew I couldn't keep going the way I was. Something had to change, and it had to change fast. The very next day, I began searching for a new role—one that would allow me to spend more time with my two beautiful daughters and redefine what success meant to me. For years, I had equated professional achievement with long hours and relentless dedication, but I now understood that success also meant being there for the people who mattered most.

The lesson wasn't an easy one to learn, and the guilt I felt at that moment was heavy. But it gave me clarity. Balance isn't something that just happens. It's a choice—a series of deliberate decisions that require constant attention.

Who I Was: The Relentless Achiever

I guess I'm here today to talk about my journey—the series of choices that shaped me into the leader I am now. A woman who, by all accounts, wasn't supposed to succeed. A woman who had the odds stacked against her and still found a way to rise.

So let's rewind a bit.

From FBI Dreams to the Corporate World

I went to college with one mission: to be Jodie Foster in *Silence of the Lambs*. I was fascinated by criminal profiling and determined to join the FBI and track down serial killers. I double-majored in psychology and sociology and minored in criminology, convinced that my path was set.

After graduation, I packed up and moved to Las Vegas, waiting for the police academy's next recruitment cycle. The goal was simple: Get a temporary job, make some money, and then step into law enforcement when the academy opened.

But life had a different plan.

I landed a job as a temp receptionist at a fast-growing telecommunications company—a role that, at first glance, seemed like a detour. But I wasn't wired to just sit at a desk and answer phones. Instead, I treated that front desk as if it were my own business. I memorized names, built relationships, and paid attention to what people needed before they even had to ask.

I quickly became the unofficial problem solver—the one people came to when they needed something done, when they needed help navigating a system, or when they just needed a moment of encouragement. I wasn't just answering phones; I was embedding myself in the fabric of the company, and people took notice.

One day, I had the chance to sit in on a training session for the customer service team. I was fascinated. It was a new enterprise-wide system rollout, and I soaked up every bit of it like a sponge. Within weeks, I had become the go-to person when someone needed help. I didn't have a formal role in training, but I was doing it anyway—helping colleagues troubleshoot, simplifying complex processes, and making things easier for those around me.

That's when a manager named John pulled me aside. He had noticed the way I naturally stepped up to support others. He made a call to the corporate Learning & Development team in Reston, Virginia, and a few weeks later, I was offered a promotion to become a corporate trainer.

The Road Warrior Years

My new job was a whirlwind. Our team was responsible for training over 5,000 employees across 60 markets in the U.S. I became a road warrior, traveling every single week. My schedule was relentless:

Fly out every Sunday.
Teach Monday through Friday.
Fly home late Friday night.
Do laundry on Saturday.
Pack up and hit the road again on Sunday.
Rinse and repeat.

It was grueling. But I loved it. I thrived on the fast pace, the challenge, and the adrenaline of being on the move. In my mind, success was directly tied to how hard I worked—the longer the hours, the more valuable I felt.

But then came love. And marriage. And a reckoning with reality.

Shifting Gears: From Trainer to Leader

I knew I couldn't start a family while living out of a suitcase. So, I took a leap and transitioned into a role at a new company—one that allowed me to shift from systems training to leadership development. Instead of teaching software, I was now coaching managers on how to lead high-performing teams—a transition that felt exhilarating but also terrifying.

Impostor syndrome hit hard.

I had never officially managed a team, and here I was, standing in front of rooms full of seasoned leaders, teaching them how to delegate, how to build trust, and how to make critical business decisions. Who was I to teach leadership?

My manager saw my doubt and called it out directly:

"Tia, you may not have direct reports, but you've led massive projects, cross-functional teams, and high-stakes initiatives. Leadership isn't just about titles—it's about impact."

That conversation changed everything. I stopped waiting for a title to validate me and started owning my influence.

Life Was Good... Until It Wasn't

By 30, my life looked picture-perfect. I was a rising star in my company, excelling in leadership development. I had two beautiful daughters—Briley and Brynna, born just 18 months apart. I had everything I had worked for.

Until my world unraveled.

My husband's health crisis started as a series of kidney stones. But it escalated into something darker—an addiction to prescription painkillers that spiraled out of control. We lived in a cycle of recovery, relapse, hope, and heartbreak. I tried to hold our family together, but addiction is relentless.

Eventually, I had to make a choice—not just for myself, but for my daughters.

I chose to walk away. I chose to be a single mom.

It was the hardest decision of my life. But it was also the beginning of a transformation I never saw coming.

The Mental Shift: Learning Resilience, Redefining Success, and Setting Boundaries

Making the decision to leave my marriage wasn't just about walking away from a relationship—it was about walking into an entirely new version of myself. For years, I had been navigating life as both a high achiever and a caretaker, stretching myself thin to meet the expectations of everyone around me. But now, the weight of single motherhood, career ambition, and emotional survival collided all at once. There was no safety net, no fallback plan—just me, my daughters, and the raw reality of rebuilding my life.

At first, survival mode kicked in. I told myself that if I just worked hard enough—if I put in the extra hours, landed the next promotion, and kept everything running smoothly—then things would feel secure again. But the truth was, I couldn't outwork my way to peace. No job title, no salary increase, and no external validation could fill the void of feeling mentally and emotionally depleted.

That was the wake-up call.

I realized that resilience wasn't about how much I could endure—it was about what I was willing to let go of. I had to unlearn the toxic belief that success was tied to exhaustion. I had spent so much time proving that I could handle everything on my own that I had never stopped to ask myself if I should.

But as I worked through these realizations, another question started gnawing at me: Where was my career heading?

Up until that point, I had spent a decade in learning and development, and I loved my work. But now that I was the sole provider for my daughters, it wasn't just about loving my job; it was about building a future that offered stability, opportunity, and long-term growth. I needed to be intentional about my next steps.

Andrew, our Vice President of HR, was responsible for every facet of human resources across our 6,000-employee global organization. One day, I walked into his office, closed the door, and asked him the question that had been on my mind for weeks: "What do I need to learn to be in your seat one day?" He didn't hesitate. "You need experience in other areas of HR," he said, listing recruiting, compensation, and benefits as essential building blocks. His answer was clear and logical, but it left me uneasy. I had spent my entire career immersed in learning and development—I knew it inside and out. Stepping into these other areas felt like uncharted territory. But I also knew he was right. If I wanted to grow—if I wanted to build the kind of career that could provide for my daughters without burning myself out—I needed to expand my expertise.

Within six months, I was applying for HR generalist roles. It was a daunting process—stepping outside my comfort zone into a role that felt unfamiliar. I finally landed a position as an HR business partner (HRBP) at a small tech firm. The job wasn't a promotion. In fact, it was a lateral move with a pay cut. But I knew it was the right decision for the long term. I wasn't chasing a title or a bigger paycheck at that moment; I was investing in my future.

Over the next few years, I gained invaluable experience across multiple facets of HR. I wasn't just learning policies and processes—

I was part of a team responsible for shaping the company's culture and creating an amazing employee experience for every person who joined the organization. I helped develop HR policies that reinforced our values, navigated complex employee relations issues, and handled high-stakes escalations with confidence. I learned the nuances of compensation strategy and saw firsthand how every HR decision had a ripple effect on engagement, retention, and overall morale.

It was a period of immense growth—professionally and personally. Looking back, I can see how pivotal that move was for my career. It wasn't the traditional upward trajectory many people equate with success, but it was the step I needed to take to build the foundation for the roles I aspired to.

That experience taught me an important lesson: Promotions and happiness don't always go hand in hand.

Sometimes, the most meaningful career moves aren't upward—they're lateral or even downward in the short term. Success isn't about chasing titles; it's about building a career that aligns with your goals and values. And sometimes, that means making trade-offs and taking risks.

I also learned that as you climb the ladder, the nature of your work changes. With higher pay and prestige often come heavier trade-offs. Understanding your own definition of fulfillment is crucial to making decisions that align with your long-term vision.

And perhaps most importantly, I learned that happiness isn't about titles—it's about living a life that reflects what matters most.

When Purpose Becomes the Foundation of Your Work

For the first time in my career, everything clicked.

Working at this small tech firm with 250 employees was the most fulfilling professional experience I had ever had. This wasn't just a job—it was a masterclass in what an extraordinary company culture could look like.

Sure, we had the fun perks—a ping-pong table in the break

room, free lunches, weekly happy hours—but those were just surface-level benefits. The real magic was in how we worked together:

- The radical candor that allowed us to give direct, honest feedback while still caring deeply about one another.
- The high-trust environment where everyone owned their responsibilities and followed through on commitments.
- The thoughtful hiring process ensured we brought in the right people—smart, talented, and fully aligned with our values.
- The strong sense of community, even as a remote workforce, where we showed up for each other in ways that extended far beyond job descriptions.

I had worked for great companies before. But this was different. This was intentional, values-driven, and high-performing in a way I had never experienced. We had a work hard, play harder mentality that didn't just drive results—it made work deeply fulfilling.

And for the first time, I had absolute clarity on my purpose: to build amazing employee experiences—ones that allowed people to love where they worked, thrive in their roles, and feel valued for their contributions.

I was professionally fulfilled. I was balanced in my life. I was thriving.

And then, the acquisition happened.

One of the largest consulting firms in the world saw us as a competitor. So, they did what massive corporations often do: They bought us out.

What happened next wasn't just an acquisition—it was a hostile takeover.

The culture we had poured our hearts into building crumbled overnight.

The new company didn't care about what had made us so successful. They weren't interested in learning about the processes we built, the tools we designed, or the magic of our employee experience. None of it mattered.

Everything we had built was stripped away—absorbed into their massive machine.

And just like that, I went from being a leader to a paper pusher. My role was reduced to receiving a spreadsheet of employee data once a week and reviewing numbers. The work I had once been so passionate about? Gone.

For the first time in my career, I felt completely disconnected from my work. I had spent years building something meaningful, something that mattered—and in an instant, it was erased.

I had lost my sense of purpose.

I told myself I would never find a company like that again. It was a once-in-a-lifetime culture, a once-in-a-lifetime role.

But I also knew I couldn't stay in a place that drained me.

The Search for Purpose—Again

I was incredibly fortunate to land at another small tech firm, this time with 400 remote employees across multiple countries. Same industry. The same kind of work I had come to love.

This time, I was stepping in as VP of Global Talent, overseeing our recruiting, learning and development, and people development teams. And from day one, I felt my purpose come back to life.

I had autonomy again. I was able to make an impact again.

- I led a refresh of our corporate values, ensuring that our purpose as a company was clear and tangible.
- We partnered with managers and leaders to build their skills and delivered programs to prepare the next generation of leadership.
- We embedded behavioral interview questions into our hiring process to ensure culture alignment with every new hire.

- We conducted quarterly engagement surveys, not just to measure employee satisfaction but to actively refine and improve the programs and policies that made our workplace truly exceptional.

But what truly set this company apart was the trust and accessibility woven into every level of the organization. The executive team wasn't just present—they were approachable, engaged, and deeply invested in both the business and the people who ran it. High trust wasn't just a concept—it was the foundation of everything we did. Employees weren't micromanaged; they were empowered. Leadership didn't operate behind closed doors; they were visible, available, and committed to transparency. We didn't just talk about work-life balance—we lived it. There was an understanding that people did their best work when they were respected, supported, and given the space to bring their whole selves to work.

Most importantly, every employee knew their purpose and impact.

And once again, I found myself saying the words I never thought I'd say again:

This is the best company I have ever worked for.

Then Came Acquisition Number Two

This one was different. It wasn't an overnight hostile takeover—it was a gradual evolution.

We were acquired by a consulting firm with 300,000 employees. And at first, things stayed the same. Business as usual. No immediate changes.

Until there were.

It started gradually—a leader leaving here, a policy changing there. New processes were introduced, aligning us more closely with the larger organization. Bit by bit, the culture began to shift. What once felt personal and agile started to feel more structured and standardized. The autonomy we had enjoyed started to give way to broader corporate frameworks.

None of these changes were sudden or unexpected in an acquisition of this scale—but collectively, over time, they reshaped the employee experience.

And then, my role changed.

I went from having full creative autonomy—being able to design and implement programs that enhanced the employee experience—to something very different:

I was now responsible for adapting our processes to align with the large firm's way of doing things.

I was no longer building culture—I was simply managing change I had no control over.

For the second time in my career, I felt the walls close in on my purpose.

And for the second time, I had to ask myself: What's next?

The Next Pivotal Moment

Losing my sense of purpose in these acquisitions forced me to confront a truth I could no longer ignore: I wasn't meant to fit into someone else's version of leadership.

I wasn't meant to adapt to cultures that didn't value what I knew to be true.

I was meant to create, build, and shape the kind of company culture and employee experience that I knew could transform organizations from the inside out.

And so, as the second acquisition unraveled the role I had once loved, I realized that it was time for something different.

Reinventing Myself at 50: The Birth of My Own Consultancy

I had spent years helping companies build extraordinary cultures—cultures where employees felt valued, where leadership was intentional, and where people could truly thrive. I had seen firsthand what worked and what didn't and the profound impact a great workplace experience had on both employees and business success.

Yet, despite all of this expertise, I found myself trapped in organizations that didn't always value the very things I knew to be true.

I had built my career on creating incredible employee experiences, but after two acquisitions that stripped away culture and reduced my work to nothing more than process management, I faced an undeniable truth: I was no longer building something. I was maintaining something that no longer aligned with me.

And that wasn't enough.

The Leap into Entrepreneurship

For years, the idea of starting my own consulting firm lingered in the back of my mind. I knew there was a massive gap in how most organizations approached culture. I had seen it time and time again —leaders knew they wanted strong engagement, high trust, and an environment where people thrived—but they didn't know how to build it.

I had spent years mastering the formula—and I knew I could help companies do better.

But leaving corporate life to go out on my own? That was terrifying.

The practical side of me knew the risks. I was almost 50, and stepping away from the comfort of a corporate paycheck wasn't something I took lightly. I had spent my entire career climbing the ranks, earning promotions, leading teams, and making an impact in well-established organizations. Entrepreneurship was an entirely different beast.

There were no promotions to chase, no corporate safety net, and no guaranteed paycheck. Just me, my experience, and the belief that I could create something meaningful—on my own terms.

The Slow Build

I didn't jump overnight. Instead, I started slowly, intentionally, and strategically.

I built a foundation for Ignite Consulting while working full-time in my corporate role.

- I wrote articles for the Forbes HR Council, sharing my insights and perspectives on workplace culture, and created several eBooks—taking all the knowledge in my head and turning it into actionable resources for leaders.
- I spoke on panels and webinars, positioning myself as an expert in the field.
- I started making intentional connections with executives at scale-up organizations, sharing my eBooks with them to test my frameworks and see the impact in real time.
- I built out my CultureCatalyst™ program, refining it until I knew it could help organizations transform their workplaces.

Bit by bit, Ignite Consulting started taking shape.
And as I did this work, something inside me came alive again.

The Fear vs. The Freedom

Stepping away from the stability of corporate life to fully embrace entrepreneurship isn't without fear.

There are moments when I second-guess myself. Moments when I wonder if I'm making a mistake by moving away from the security of a well-defined career path. Moments when I think: What if this fails?

But then, there are also moments of pure exhilaration.

I imagine a future where I'm no longer building someone else's vision—I'm shaping my own.

I'm no longer trying to fit my expertise into a box that doesn't align with my values.

I'm no longer playing by corporate rules that undervalue the human side of business.

I know that my true purpose isn't just about climbing the corporate ladder—it's about helping organizations transform their cultures in a way that actually matters.

And the more I lean into that purpose, the more I feel something I haven't in a long time:

Freedom.

What I Learned About Leadership, Success, and Balance

This journey taught me lessons that no corporate role ever could:

- **Leadership isn't about titles—it's about impact.** For years, I thought I had to be in a senior leadership position to drive change. But true leadership is about influence, not hierarchy.
- **Success isn't about climbing the ladder—it's about alignment.** The best career move isn't always up—sometimes, it's sideways, backward, or completely off the path you thought you were supposed to follow.
- **Balance isn't a luxury—it's a choice.** Building Ignite Consulting allowed me to create the life I had always envisioned—a fulfilling career that didn't come at the cost of my well-being.

Now, I wake up every day doing work that aligns with my values, challenges me, and allows me to make a real difference.

A New Chapter

Reinventing myself at 50 wasn't just about starting a business. It was about taking control of my future. It was about choosing fulfillment over familiarity. It was about proving that it's never too late to step into your true purpose.

And if I've learned anything, it's this: You don't have to stay on a path just because you've walked it for years. You can choose a new one. And sometimes, that's where the real success begins.

The Bigger Picture: Redefining Leadership

For most of my career, I believed leadership meant sacrifice—long hours, relentless commitment, and putting work above everything else. Busyness became a badge of honor, as if the harder I worked, the more valuable I was.

But that version of leadership is broken.

I sacrificed time with my daughters.

I worked myself into exhaustion.

I let my identity become wrapped up in my career.

And yet, when I lost my purpose, I found a new understanding of leadership—one that doesn't require burnout as proof of ambition.

A New Leadership Standard: Balance Over Burnout

For years, women have been told that success comes at a cost—that we must prove our worth through exhaustion, say yes to everything, and fit into a leadership model that was never designed with us in mind.

But I've learned that true leadership isn't about doing it all—it's about doing what matters most.

- Leadership is about presence, not just productivity. The best leaders aren't the busiest; they're the ones who focus on what truly drives impact.
- Leadership is about boundaries, not burnout. Saying no isn't a weakness—it's a leadership skill.

- Leadership is about alignment, not obligation. Success isn't just about climbing the ladder—it's about building a career that fits your life, not the other way around.

The best leaders don't just lead with vision—they model the way forward.

The Responsibility of Leading Differently

As women, we often feel an invisible pressure to be everything to everyone: a high-performing professional, a present and engaged mother, a supportive friend, mentor, and leader.

And for too long, we've been told that success means making it work at all costs.

But how we lead teaches others what's possible.

If we burn ourselves out, we send the message that exhaustion is the price of ambition.

If we say yes to everything, we reinforce the idea that saying no is a failure.

If we equate success with stress, we teach the next generation that thriving is optional.

I refuse to be part of that cycle.

I want my daughters to know that being successful doesn't mean being depleted.

I want the women I mentor to see that balance isn't a luxury—it's a choice.

I want leaders to understand that a thriving culture starts with leading by example.

Because if we don't define success for ourselves, someone else will do it for us.

LIMITLESS LEADERSHIP

A Call to Redefine Leadership

We live in a world that glorifies hustle over health, urgency over intention, and sacrifice over sustainability. But what if we stop measuring success by how much we can endure?

What if we challenge the outdated norms that tell us we have to choose between success and balance?

What if we decide that we don't have to burn out to prove our worth?

The Legacy We Leave Behind

> I've held incredible leadership roles.
> I've built high-performing teams.
> I've helped transform organizations.
> But the most important leadership role I've ever had?
> Being a mother.

When my daughters look back on the life I built, I don't want them to remember a woman who was always too busy, too tired, or too distracted by work.

I want them to remember a mother who built a career on her own terms. Who showed them that leadership isn't about burnout—it's about balance. Who proved that success and fulfillment don't have to be in opposition.

Rather than telling you how they see me, I'll let them speak for themselves.

Briley, age 20:

> *Over the past 20 years, my mom has taught me countless lessons: how to color inside the lines, ride a bike, enhance my essays with stronger adjectives, drive a car, live independently, and even file my taxes. But the most profound lesson—and one I know I'll continue learning for years to come—is how to build a life you're genuinely excited to wake up to.*

My mom, one of the most humble people I know, has guided our family through seasons of scarcity to moments of abundance, from empty pockets to buying my first car. Her success wasn't achieved by following the crowd or succumbing to societal norms. Instead, she took control of her life, trusted in her worth, and worked tirelessly to create a future she could be proud of.

Some may know her as a vice president, author, leader, or boss. But to me, she's always been "Mom" first—and that role outweighs all other titles combined.

In 10, 20, even 30 years, if I can become even half the person my mother is, I'll know I'm on the right path. Her leadership and unwavering confidence have not only shaped her life but mine as well, and I am endlessly grateful for the example she continues to set.

Brynna, age 18:

If you asked me how I truly see my mom, this is what I would tell you.

She is my best friend in the whole world—the strongest woman I know. I couldn't do anything without her.

I would tell you about how she took two little girls and raised them into strong, capable women and how she has always been committed to my well-being and cares deeply about where I end up in life. She has stood by my side countless times, even when I've disappointed her.

I would tell you how much it upsets me when I get mad at her because I know she always has my best interest at heart. She will stay up all night just to comfort me when I'm struggling.

She is the only one who can truly calm me down during my worst panic attacks.

I would tell you how much care and patience she shows me, no matter what stage of life I'm in. She has helped me through every heartbreak. She has never stopped believing in me and my future—even in the moments when I struggled to believe in myself.

I would tell you about her faith—how she always goes to church with me, how she baptized me, and how she leads by example in ways that shape my own faith.

I would tell you that she is the hardest worker I've ever met. She gives everything to me and my sister without hesitation. That she is the most selfless person I know.

I would tell you how much I think about her throughout the day. How grateful I am for every moment she's been there for me.

And then, I would tell you about my fear—my fear of having children one day because I don't know how I could ever live up to the kind of mother she is.

I would tell you that I would be absolutely nowhere in life without her. I can't imagine a world without her love, her strength, and her unwavering support.

And most of all, I would tell you that God truly blessed me with the best mother in the world.

The Final Shift: Leadership on Your Terms

We all have a choice.

We can continue playing by the old rules, where success is measured by how much we give up.

Or we can write our own rules, proving that fulfillment and achievement can coexist.

Because here's what I know for sure: When we stop glorifying burnout, we make space for innovation, creativity, and sustainability.

When we stop wearing exhaustion as a badge of honor, we become better leaders, better parents, better partners, and better people.

When we stop chasing someone else's version of success, we find the freedom to create our own.

And that's the leadership legacy I want to leave behind.

So, my challenge to you is this:

What kind of leader do you want to be?

The choice is yours.

Tia Smith is a corporate culture strategist, HR and talent expert, and published author dedicated to helping organizations build thriving, people-centric workplaces. As the founder of Ignite Consulting, she partners with CEOs and executive leaders of scale-up organizations to create high-performance cultures that drive engagement, retention, and long-term success.

A dedicated mother and mentor, Tia is known for her authenticity, resilience, and commitment to redefining leadership through balance, purpose, and intentionality. With over 25 years of experience in HR, leadership development, and talent strategy, she has led large-scale cultural transformations and helped organizations align their values, people, and business objectives.

In addition to her consulting work, Tia is a sought-after speaker, delivering keynotes and panel discussions on healthy workplace culture, leadership, and work-life balance.

Passionate about helping leaders build workplaces where employees feel valued and empowered, Tia believes that a strong culture isn't just a perk—it's a competitive advantage.

If you're ready to transform your company culture and unlock your organization's full potential, visit www.igniteyourculture.io to explore how we can work together. Let's make it happen!

Connect with Tia

🌐 Website
www.igniteyourculture.io

🔗 LinkedIn
https://www.linkedin.com/in/tiasmith/